Creative Financing
of Real Estate

James A. Misko

Creative Financing of Real Estate

James A. Misko

Institute for Business Planning

INSTITUTE FOR BUSINESS PLANNING, Inc.
IBP Plaza • Englewood Cliffs, N.J. 07632

"This publication is designed to provide accurate and authoritative information in regard to the subject matter covered. It is sold with the understanding that the publisher is not engaged in rendering legal, accounting or other professional service. If legal advice is required, the services of a competent professional person should be sought."

—*From a Declaration of Principles jointly adopted by a Committee of the American Bar Association and a Committee of Publishers and Associations.*

Second Printing . . . . . December, 1981

© Copyright 1981, by Institute for Business Planning, Inc.
IBP Plaza, Englewood Cliffs, N.J. 07632

All rights reserved. No part of this book may be reproduced in any form or by any means, without permission in writing from the publisher.

Library of Congress Cataloging in Publication Data

Misko, James A.
    Creative financing of real estate.

    1. Real estate business--Finance.   I. Title.
HD1375.M49   332.7'2   81-6329
ISBN 0-87624-108-9   AACR2

Printed in the United States of America

Dedication

Nobody reads dedications in books. They are communications between the authors and the few people mentioned in them. Anyone not mentioned will be hard put to realize that the book was in some part dedicated to him or her.

Sitting down at the typewriter to write, and doing it fairly and honestly, a writer knows that what goes on the pages comes from his total experience with life—and no one person, no mere handful of people, should receive that dedication.

Rather it is to all people who touched the author and made him what he was when he wrote it, that a book should be dedicated. Some gave him support, some shunned him. Some laughed and hunted and swore with him. Some hated him, some loved him. Some cared and some didn't give a damn.

To all of those fine souls who moved me in one direction or another, whether they know it or not, this book is dedicated.

Jim Misko

Acknowledgments

I want to thank Tami for her diligent typing of this manuscript, above and beyond the fact that she had to do it

Also to my wife Patti, who rearranged the room upstairs so that I could write with the view of the Turnagain Arm and the limitless panorama of the Alaska Range. She also read downstairs while I typed upstairs, which is not a fun way of doing things together.

About the Author

James A. Misko has written and lectured widely on creative financing and other aspects of real estate. He entered the real estate profession in Oregon in 1960 at the age of twenty-eight, and after two years of selling houses branched out into real estate specialties. Included among his specialties are investment sales, leasing, property management, construction and development, exchanging, counseling and syndication.

Misko has long been in the forefront of innovative real estate financing. In the mid-1960s, well before "creative financing" became a byword among real estate professionals, he published a booklet entitled *Creative Financing of Real Estate*. In it he outlined unusual methods of financing real estate transactions. This booklet led to speaking engagements and eventually grew into a national seminar on "Creative Financing in Real Estate." The seminar has been held in twenty-one states and remains *the* course in creative financing. Misko has also spoken at local, state and national real estate conventions and has contributed articles to national real estate publications.

Since 1974, Misko has lived in Anchorage, Alaska, and divides his time between syndications and development. He is a charter Certified Commercial Investment member of the Realtors National Marketing Institute and has served as an instructor for this organization. Misko has also held elected posts in local, state and national realtors organizations.

Creative Financing of Real Estate is based on the original booklet which helped launch Misko's many speaking engagements on the subject of creative financing. *Creative Financing* has been expanded and updated to meet the needs of today's real estate climate. Misko writes about creative financing like he talks it and lives it. The techniques described in this book are not theories but workable, usable financing methods that have been put to the test in actual practice. Now Misko shares these techniques with you as he has shared them with others.

What This Book Will Do For You

It took dozens of top real estate professionals years to devise the fifty deal-closing financing secrets outlined in *Creative Financing of Real Estate*. Now, Jim Misko has put them all together in an easy-to-use guide that will help you put the financial wraps on virtually any real estate deal, and also help you put thousands of dollars in your pocket. Stripped bare of theory and wasted words, *Creative Financing of Real Estate* gives you nothing but the straight facts and techniques you need to get buyers and sellers together in today's tight-money, high-interest real estate market.

If you have to look outside the mainstream for real estate financing—and these days, who doesn't?—you'll want to keep this guide within easy reach at all times. This book can teach you.

- How to use financing techniques developed and time-tested by the pros—techniques such as "The Rainy Day Option," "The Ultimate Bail Out," and "The Velvet Hammer" that turns a leaseback into a triple-A guaranteed leased property.
- How and when to use each financing method, in-

cluding examples to demonstrate how these creative techniques can be put to work in actual practice.
- How to generate badly-need cash . . . how to option a property without money . . . how to get 100 percent financing . . . how to buy, option, sell and exchange real estate paper.
- How you can build a personal fortune by exchanging your property tax-free.
- The real way to get sellers to stand behind the figures they give for their property.
- How owner financing can help you buy the house of your dreams.
- How to get a lender to grant you a loan he wouldn't ordinarily make.
- How you can put a frozen equity to work in a tight money market by creating real estate paper.
- How you can wind up a winner by turning your dwindling stocks into real estate equities.
- Tax strategies in creative financing that help you hang onto more of your earnings and give as little as legally possible to Uncle Sam.

Whether you're buying, selling or exchanging real estate on your own behalf or for your clients, *Creative Financing of Real Estate* can help you put the deal together in almost any market. If you are a real estate investor, you'll no longer have to watch helplessly while the deal of a lifetime slips through your fingers for lack of financing. If you are a broker or financial advisor, *Creative Financing of Real Estate* will give you financing ideas to help clients set up low cash and no cash deals. These deals could help you earn thousands of dollars in additional commissions. You'll refer to *Creative Financing of Real Estate* again and again for help in solving your toughest real estate financing problems.

A Word From the Author

During most of the past thirty-five years you could count on certain real estate and financing truths. One of those truths was that there would be money available to finance almost everything at a reasonable rate over a reasonable period of time. This truth was exploded during the 1973–1974 and 1979–1980 recessions, when employment, coupled with a nationwide recession and double-digit inflation, forced the government to borrow heavily from the private funds, thus creating chaos in the money market and uncertainty in real estate financing. Interest rates moved from 10 percent to 20 percent in a few months, and loans that used to be taken for granted (such as refinancing your home to obtain business capital) were no longer available.

Because of this degree of uncertainty, I've been forced to include certain words in this text—words such as "generally," or "often," or "in general,"—that would not be there but for current market conditions. I've used these words to qualify some of the financing techniques I've described, because some of these techniques may not work in your marketplace at the exact moment you read about them.

The fact that the exact circumstances may not be workable at a given moment does not mean that you can't profit from them. For one thing, market conditions change, and what may not work today may work very well tomorrow. For another, one key to creative financing is to adapt techniques to existing market conditions. The techniques presented here were developed by some very creative people who did not rest there. Instead, they polished their techniques, refined them and used them in differing circumstances, until they became extremely valuable tools for creating high earnings. Each technique is but the tip of an iceberg of knowledge, and variations still unused wait beneath the surface to be discovered.

                                                  James A. Misko

Contents

Dedication v
Acknowledgments vii
About the Author ix
What This Book Will Do for You xi

A Word From the Author xiii

1. How to Own a Champagne House on a Beer Income 1
2. Postdate Sale to Secure One Property While
   Selling Another 5
3. How to Support a Small Down Payment by Using
   Collateral Security 7
4. How to Fund with Life Insurance to Support a Contract 11
5. How to Use a Life Estate to Obtain the Property
   You Want 13
6. How to Use a Life Insurance Annuity to Develop
   Cash Flow for the Elderly Seller 17
7. How to Gain Appreciation and Working Time by
   Using an Option to Purchase 19
8. How to Option Property Without Money 23
9. The Rainy Date Option: How to Reap Riches
   Tomorrow by Paying a Higher Price Today 25

10. Split the Fee and Carve Up the Benefits for Investors 29
11. Trade One Set of Benefits for Another by Exchanging Instead of Buying 31
12. How to Get the Twin Benefits of Tax Shelter and Spendable Income Through an Overtrade and Cashback ... 35
13. How to Exchange and Borrow to Get Your Assets Working for You 37
14. How to Have Your Cake and Eat It Later 39
15. Creation of Paper: How to Put a Frozen Equity to Work in a Tight Money Market 43
16. How to Buy, Option, Sell, and Exchange Paper 47
17. How Exchanging Paper Can Generate a Steady Cash Flow 57
18. How to Buy Property for 20 Percent Off While the Seller Gets His Asking Price 61
19. How to Use the Broker's Fee in Financing the Transaction .. 65
20. Financing Financed Raw Land: How to Get out of "Eat" and Maintain Appreciation 69
21. Payments Don't Always Include Principal and Interest— and Sometimes Not Even Interest 73
22. The Many Advantages of Separating the Down Payment From the Principal 77
23. How to Convert Principal Payments to Tax Deductible Lease Payments 81
24. How to Acquire Land With No Cash 83
25. How to Get 100 Percent Financing Via a Sale and Leaseback 87
26. The Velvet Hammer: How to Turn a Leaseback Into a Triple-A Guaranteed Leased Property 91
27. Sale and Buyback—and Exchange and Buyback 95
28. How to Create Cash By Discount Sale and Lease Option— and Still Retain the Benefits of the Property 99
29. The Blanket Mortgage: How to Secure a Favorable Loan by Using More Than One Property 103
30. The Wrap-Around: How to Secure New Financing Without Disturbing Existing Financing 107

Table of Contents

31. How to Syndicate the Loan and Get More Than One Lender in the Picture 111
32. C.D. for Loan: How to Get a Lender to Make a Loan He Wouldn't Ordinarily Make 115
33. Raise the Interest and Lower the Price 119
34. Lender Loans 75 Percent of Appraisal or Sales Price— or Does He? 123
35. Performance Mortgage: How to Base Your Payments on the Performance of the Property 127
36. Performance Purchase Price: The Real Way to Get the Seller to Stand Behind the Figures He Gives for His Property 131
37. Such a Business—You Got It—You Sell It—And You've Still Got It! 135
38. Convertible Loan to Equity: A Way to Give the Lender an Incentive to Make the Loan 139
39. Convertible Loan to Stock: How to Motivate a Lender to Make a Corporate Loan 143
40. Marry an Investor to a User 147
41. Working Out of Tough Sale or Lease Terms 149
42. How to Make Owner Financing Work for You 153
43. How to Push the Second Mortgage Around to Get the Property You Want 159
44. How to Make the Second Mortgage Bring in Cash 161
45. How to Get Cash by Solving Someone Else's Problem 163
46. How to Wind Up a Winner by Turning Your Dwindling Stocks Into Real Estate Equities 167
47. The Ultimate Bail Out 171
48. Never Use a Dollar Once 177
49. Interest and Points 149
50. Tax Strategies in Creative Financing 187
    Selected Real Estate Tables 195

1

How to Own a Champagne House on a Beer Income

This plan is designed to help a homeowner buy an even nicer home at no extra cost. It involves a sale and an exchange, and it requires a client who has confidence in your ability to perform the necessary functions.

Let's say your client has a $60,000 house and he is earning $30,000 a year in personal income. He and his family want to own an $80,000 house, but they feel their income does not provide them with enough left over after expenses to cover the increased payments. They have, however, found an $80,000 home they like, their credit is good, and they have a good equity (20 percent to 50 percent) in their $60,000 home.

Know How Item

Take your client to his banker and borrow $15,000 for the down payment on the $80,000 house. Figure out the amount that it will cost him over what he is paying now on the $60,000 home. Then exchange his equity in the $60,000 home into an apartment house with enough spendable income to pay the difference and repay the $15,000 to the bank in payments. He now has the $80,000 home he and his family wanted and enough spendable income from the apartments to cover the increased payments and repay the loan at the bank. He also has a depreciation allowance on the apartments that lowers his ordinary income tax. He will probably need that tax savings to repay the loans.

Example

A realtor friend of mine had a client who owned a home appraised at $60,000. He owed $9,500 balance at $100 per month. The client had been in the same job for ten years, his children were in high school, and his family had come to the conclusion that they wanted a larger home in a better area. When they figured it out on a budget, they just couldn't manage to squeeze out enough to make the additional $360 a month it would take to pay for the home they wanted. Nevertheless, they looked at the home several times and after a month, when no one else had bought it, they came to the realtor with open minds.

They told him they would do anything reasonable to get that home. He analyzed their problem and then ascertained that the man's credit was spotless; verified his income and job security; and he discussed with the homeowners the possibilities of a contract sale.

Then he returned to his client and laid out the plan that was accepted and implemented. He asked his client to meet him at his bank the next day where they negotiated for a $15,000 loan. The broker presented the $15,000 to the $100,000 homeowners as the down payment on a contract sale and carried back his fee to be paid from the contract payments.

Next, he took the $60,000 house that his clients wanted to vacate and exchanged it with a builder who had a twelve-unit apartment house that would show a spendable income of $300 a month after all expenses and amortization of the new contract. The broker took his fee back to be paid from the contract payments of the apartments.

The first year's taxable loss on the apartments was $7,410, which reduced the client's taxable income enough to save him an additional $1,556 in taxes. The spendable income of $300 a month plus the savings of $1,556 in taxes was enough to let the client live in the $100,000 house and make no more payment out of his ordinary income than he was paying to live in the $60,000 house.

2

Postdate Sale to Secure One Property While Selling Another

One of the easiest techniques to understand and use is the postdated sale. Your client is selling a piece of property to get enough cash to purchase a property he either needs or wants more than the one he has. You offer an exchange, which the seller refuses. He will not wait while you complete a series of exchanges to give him the money he wants. He is a typical seller—"Give me cash or forget it!"

Know How Item

Advise your client to sign an earnest money receipt offering to purchase the property of Mr. Typical Seller with a postdated completion of escrow date. Ninety to 180 days is usually enough. Generally that is all the seller will hold still for unless your offer is extremely sweet with cash or price.

This means, of course, that both you and your client must now back up your statements about your client's property, because you must produce within the time limit or forfeit the earnest money. On most earnest money forms there is a clause that states in effect: "If the purchaser does not comply with the conditions of the earnest money receipt he forfeits his earnest money." You should explain this to the seller and also probably make some arrangement with him for the distribution of the funds if the buyer does default. But he won't default because you are now working with two clients who are working twenty-four hours a day to help you sell the property in the time limit. Use your clients. Tell them to talk to people about real estate wherever they go and specifically about the property that is on the market. They should be sure to mention the realtor with whom the property is listed.

Example

A razzle-dazzle client of mine is often prone to handling his own real estate, especially when it comes to buying, since he often looks for properties that I do not handle. He wanted a particular farm very badly, and he was convinced that a major road would go through the property in the future. The client was not flush with money and he had tried every exchange offer he could muster—all with no success. At last he plunked down $500 for earnest money providing he could have ninety days to sell some property he had and pay the cash the seller required. It was accepted.

Between the farmer and my client the property was exposed at every grange meeting, political meeting, council meeting, and any other meeting that would stand for the intrusion. It sold within the ninety day period and the purchase was consummated.

3

How to Support a Small Down Payment by Using Collateral Security

---

How many times have you heard your seller say, "He isn't putting enough down." In many instances you may have a buyer who wants a property, has good security to pay the mortgage or contract, and holds a good job. The owner wants to sell badly, but the thought of receiving too small a down payment is enough to kill the earnest money. You have a willing seller and a willing buyer—all you need to close is the financing.

Know How Item

Often the buyer owns his car, furniture, livestock, guns, boat, trailer house, or something of value free and clear or with considerably greater worth than the present encumbrances. You write a chattel mortgage on the items with enough security to make the seller feel his transaction is strong. Release the chattel after a certain amount has been paid on the principal.

If more money must be added later, arrange for a payoff on the chattel, but arrange the payoff of the chattel to fit whatever you encumber. If it is a car or boat, make it easy on the buyer—monthly or quarterly payments if they fit his financial situation. If it is livestock or something that he intends to market at some future date, make the payment due a reasonable time after usual market time. This also works on crops that will be marketed in the future.

If the amount needed is $1,500 or less, you can finance almost anybody through a small-loan company. The interest is high but they will carry three years or more on security and if cash is important to the transaction and your buyer is really motivated, use it.

Know How Item

Another method of providing security for a small down payment is to pledge other paper, either contracts, mortgages, or stocks and bonds that the buyer does not wish to get rid of—or the seller is not willing to accept on the purchase or exchange. These can be forfeited in the event of default to the seller. The income from contracts or mortgages or personal note collections can often be pledged as additional security.

The number of things that you can use for collateral security is limited only by your imagination, the buyer's or exchanger's assets, and his willingness to use them to gain the benefits of ownership of the seller's property

Example

My office had a young estate building client who wanted a $60,000 commercial property listed with another broker. We offered to exchange a $20,000 second paper on the property, but the old owner felt that the possibilities of default on the $20,000 paper were stronger than he wished to tie into. This was coupled with the fact that the owner wished to retire trouble-free, consequently the offer was rejected. After consultation with my client, I presented an offer for nothing down on the $60,000 property and used the $20,000 second contract as collateral security that would be forfeited if my client defaulted on his contract with the seller. It was accepted. The owner subsequently retired in his trailer house. The payments have been made to escrow promptly out of the income from the $60,000 property. The buyer enjoys the additional security of $200 a month from the $20,000 paper to cover him in case of vacancy or lower rents.

4

How to Fund With Life Insurance to Support a Contract

Many people in the real estate market do not have extremely strong financial statements. Most depend on their income for their survival. Almost all have had no estate planning. If their income were to stop because of death, illness or accident, their real estate investments could come to an end, especially if their properties did not produce enough income to cover all expenses including a manager.

There is reason for many sellers to doubt the buyer's ability to continue paying for the property if the buyer has an accident, severe illness, or dies prematurely. The insurance companies have provided a myriad of policies to cure almost any of these situations—for a price.

Know How Item

If your buyer can pass the physical examination for insurance, then you can have him buy a sickness and accident policy that will provide enough money to cover the payments on the property he is purchasing, even if his income is shut off. These can be assigned to the seller in the event the payments are not made.

If the seller is worried about what will happen to his property payments in the event of death, the best solution is to provide decreasing term insurance to cover the amount of the mortgage or contract as it pays off. There are some insurance agents who are sharp enough to devise an ordinary life policy for your buyer which, by borrowing the cash value as it accumulates, will create a larger estate and leave the buyer with a usable policy after the need to cover the mortgage has passed. This can be done for almost the same cost to your buyer as term insurance and will be more valuable in the end.

Mortgage cancellation insurance can be obtained to pay off the mortgage completely when death occurs. This will cover the cost of the property 100 percent if necessary. This need not add to the monthly payments, but it can be added on to the end of the mortgage. In the event he sells or trades the property, the escrow agent charges for the time the coverage was used. Very painless at the time of the original transaction.

Example

A fifty-year-old doctor was a long-time client of mine. Although he made a good income, he had not spent much on building his estate. His income taxes had become unbearable, and he needed our help. Out of our listings we had a client who needed to raise cash by the sale of an apartment building. Our offer was accepted on the condition that we provide insurance to cover the purchase money mortgage that the seller took back on the apartments. The doctor had no health problems and breezed through the physical examination. We obtained $35,000 worth of life insurance on a decreasing term basis that covered the mortgage in the event of the doctor's death and that went down in value with the mortgage. With the doctor's high income the premium was easy to pay and well worth it because, if he died, the property would be paid down to the first mortgage and would provide his family with $500 a month spendable income.

5

How to Use a Life Estate to Obtain the Property You Want

There are many people who believe sincerely that they should not leave their children anything. They have worked hard all their lives, have earned a goodly amount and their children have been provided for. Or, perhaps there are no children, only the elderly couple. Maybe the couple is not so elderly. There are many situations that a life estate fits, and it is not wise to rule any of them out.

Generally, however, I have seen the life estate work in the case of older people who have a house sitting on greatly appreciated land, something fit for multiple-family or commercial use. Assume that a developer has his eye on it, but the old people are not interested in money or another house. Oh, they would take another house if it was just like the one they are in now and within two blocks of downtown. Well, you know it is ridiculous to look for something like that—that's what you are trying to get from them.

The developer has several apartment houses and some duplexes that you have vainly tried to exchange to this couple. They would like to live in one, but the problems of ownership, even if you manage it, are too heavy for them to contemplate.

Know How Item

Pick the unit they would like to live in and take them to your attorney. Draw up a life estate in one of the apartment or duplex units, giving them the right to live there as long as either of them lives. If the wife is much younger, you might get them to understand the life estate would have to be with the older husband, but that is between you and your developer. You will need to figure the loss of revenue and the loss of value if he sells it with the life estate on it. Sometimes a free-and-clear piece of land at the right time is worth much more to a developer if it enables him to build at the right time and finance it properly.

Example

A developer who was nobody's client and everybody's prospect was searching for commercial land on which to build an office building. Another realtor and I put together a parcel large enough for the developer's needs in the area he wanted. After hours of talking and of presenting alternate offers, we found out that all the owners really wanted was for their property to provide them with a free living for the rest of their lives. Overjoyed with their answer, we rushed back to the developer and obtained his permission to write them a life estate for as long as either of them lived in a duplex unit he owned.

He had built the duplex unit ten years earlier and it was not as modern as the new ones, but that appealed to the older sellers because it was more like home. The developer's cost was low in the building and he had taken heavy depreciation in the early years, something that hindered selling it now. Since it was not an expensive duplex, his cost in it was low and his book basis was low, he decided it would be worth putting that property on ice. In other words, he decided to use the depreciation and let the one side pay off the existing mortgage balance in order to get the commercial land free and clear.

It so happened that after five years the husband died and the wife wanted to get out of the duplex. The developer was in a better cash position now, and he bought out the widow's life estate and she moved in with her daughter. At the right time and the right place it solved everyone's problems.

6

How to Use a Life Insurance Annuity to Develop Cash Flow for the Elderly Seller

This is probably the least-used method of financing. It takes cash, and that requires a well-capitalized buyer or a good financial statement in order to borrow enough from the bank to buy the annuity outright

I have seen it work with older people as sellers. They had enough to live on and wanted the property to provide them with a certain added income for the rest of their lives.

Know How Item

Using tables, any life insurance salesman can show you what amount of money it would take to buy an annuity to provide a certain income for a person of a certain age. If the seller is close to the retirement age, this can often work if understood and used by the realtor.

Twenty-three thousand four hundred dollars ($23,400) will provide $200 a month for the lifetime of a man aged 60 at the time it is purchased. In other words, your buyer pays $23,400 cash to a life insurance company, which in turn invests the money and pays the seller $200 a month during his lifetime.

Example

An elderly carpetlayer had listed his property with another broker. After a long period of asking too much for the property, he got out of the listing and complained that he couldn't sell because capital gains taxes would eat up so much of his profit. His property had a fair market value of $30,000, but he wanted $40,000 if he sold and he wouldn't sell for less. However, he wanted to be rid of the responsibility for the property. What he wanted was a monthly income of $200 from it.

A corporation needed the land, but would not pay $40,000 for it. The seller would not sell. With $23,400 in cash, the corporation bought him an annuity that paid him $200 per month for his lifetime. He paid taxes, assured that his monthly income was not hampered by poor management, turns in the economy, death of anybody or dissolution of the corporation. He smiled all the way to Southern California.

7

How to Gain Appreciation and Working Time by Using an Option to Purchase

The option to purchase is not often used as a financing tool. It is generally thought of as a tool to tie up the seller of a property while you go about solving problems of zoning, putting together more parcels, finding leases or solving any other problem that is blocking your path to immediate development.

The option is, however, one of the least expensive methods of controlling property available. You pay no taxes, generally no interest, no principal, and no carrying charges. If you can control people and property for less than that, drop me a line about it.

Know How Item

One of the best uses of an option for financing is when you are trying to put a syndicate or corporation together to purchase a piece of property and you need time to solicit the prospective members. With a ten dollar bill you can option the property. The owner will be happy that the terms and conditions have been agreed upon and there is nothing remaining now but for him to sit back and wait for you to perform—which you will, having proved the feasibility of the thing to yourself and others beforehand.

If you have chosen the location well and it is close to development time, a rise in market value may occur during the period you hold the option. This is especially true if you buy on an upswing in the market. This accrues to you and, in effect, gives you equity position, even though you have only ten dollars cash in it. Occasionally you can option for six months to a year for small amounts of cash and with inflation, you have increased its value by 2.5 percent or more without paying taxes, interest or insurance.

Example

I had looked at a particular corner for over a year, thinking what a good office location it would make. After awhile I looked up the owners and approached them to sell. They were willing and I made an offer. They countered it by asking for more cash than I could muster, and they wouldn't come down in their cash requirements. We spent much time on the deal, until finally it was simply a matter of my not having enough cash to buy the lot. I knew others would like the location as much as I did, so I requested an option for ninety days to work it out. They agreed. I extended the option another ninety days when I had not completed assembling the group I needed. At the end of six months we were still short of having the necessary capital. It was not that people were not available, but the investors I brought in did not want any one large stockholder. We were approaching people of limited means who hemmed and hawed about it due to its total dollar value and their small resources.

After the seventh month we dropped the option, unable to get enough people together to do the job. The owner was a bit discouraged for several months. Then the city acquired the adjacent block for the construction of a new city hall, and the owner was all smiles. He raised his price from $4 to $7 a square foot and got it within the year. If we had gotten our group together, the option would have served as interim financing to hold the property and gain us equity while we constructed our organization.

8

How to Option a Property Without Money

Able owns a property you want, and he is actively trying to market it. He needs a sale, and he needs to get out of the liability for the loan on the property. So far, no one has made him an offer that he can't refuse and he sits there with his property—while you want it.

Know How Item

What do you have that Able might accept as option consideration? He may not need other things, but he may want them and he may take them. There is no telling the motivations of a seller. A good buyer should be able to use anything he isn't holding for long term to acquire real estate.

You can offer personal property for an option—notes, a car, stock you have that isn't doing so well, paintings, guns, jewelry. You can create a note and trust deed against other property you own. Offer one or more of these items to the seller as an option consideration.

Offer other real estate for an option. This could be a lot, or rental, an equity in a house or income property. You can offer other interests in real estate such as a limited partnership interest, a lease, or rents from real estate. It doesn't have to be money. Any of the items mentioned here can serve as consideration and Able might be willing to accept any one of them. It benefits him to take something. You just need to find out what it is that turns him on. All you need to make it work is to arrive at a sum that satisfies you and him.

Example

A builder had plans for a duplex and he thought the market was right. He needed to firm up his financing and wanted to acquire some duplex lots now before the market opened in the spring. But he lacked cash to bind any agreement. He had several properties in his "keeper" inventory that were almost paid off, had old 6 percent loans on them, were in good condition and always rented. One duplex in particular had a low loan and rentals of $225 per side. He needed about seven month's time before the beginning of spring construction.

He offered the rents from one side of the duplex as option consideration on six duplex lots for seven months. That amounted to $1,575 which was deducted from the purchase price when the transaction closed. It was accepted. Both parties were happy.

9

The Rainy Day Option: How to Reap Riches Tomorrow By Paying a Higher Price Today

---

You have some excess cash or property and what you are really trying to do is get some meaningful benefits about ten years down the road. You have looked at various parcels of land; several commercial buildings; and an in-town quarter block that has an old magnificent residence on it. They are all priced above the present market value however, and although they are getting a lot of looker interest, nobody is buying.

The owners of these parcels don't really care. They are not strongly motivated to sell or they would have priced them at today's market price. But in your heart of hearts, you feel that several of these parcels of property will do great things in the next ten years.

Know How Item

The object of the rainy day option is to pay above today's price. *But*, the way to to it is to offer about 10 percent of the asking price as an option for ten years. Use your cash and/or property as the option consideration. Offer price and terms at the seller's price, but do it by asking for a ten-year option.

During the ten years you have no holding costs. The idea is that the appreciation will move this "winner" property into a great deal of profit. You will benefit while the others who would not pay the seller's asking price will be behind. The seller? He will have a wonderful ego trip because he "sold" his property at tomorrow's price today.

Go back and look at properties you could have purchased ten years ago and didn't because they were priced too high. Recalculate what you might have made had you given in to that price but used the option instead.

If you can't get a full ten-year option, you might offer amounts of money at various times to extend the option. Maybe 5 percent to 10 percent in a few years.

I know an enterprising fellow in Idaho who options for two to three years, generally on land parcels he wants to subdivide. He pays from 10 percent to 15 percent of the asking price as option money. During the two years he does his planning, engineering, some pre-sales of smaller land parcels (often selling off the house and buildings with a five to twenty acre parcel to get more cash to help close the sale) and then closes the transaction by exercising the option.

Several times he has had to extend the option period and has paid an additional 5 percent to extend another year.

Example

In our goal to provide benefits later by paying a higher price today, let's examine a living example.

A local doctor owned a house located one block from the business zoning. His use was residential. He often needed money to support other business investments. The asking price on his house was out of this world according to residential salespeople. Let's use the figures. His house was valued by him at $240,000. It was probably "worth" $150,000, but it had two interesting angles to it. It was across the street from a state-built home for senior citizens, and it was very close to business zoning.

Astute planning could have told you an option would work. The owner always needed money, the location was excellent, the property was overpriced and therefore unsalable in the current market.

Five years later, the state condemned the doctor's house in order to expand the senior citizens home and paid him $750,000 for it. He wanted $1,000,000. Had you optioned it five years ago for $25,000, where would you have been?

10

Split the Fee and Carve Up the Benefits for Investors

Often a solution to your client's problem is unobtainable because of the high cost of the property that would meet his needs. He needs depreciation badly to cover ordinary income, or he wants long-term, safe investment with a solid return. Somewhere along the way you've probably located the vehicle for his investment ideas but everything you have found has been too high priced for him, or the safety was not there, or it took more management than he wanted to give.

Know How Item

Split the fee on a property. If he is looking for maximum depreciation, sell him the building only and lease him the land. Then sell the land to another person looking for safe investment with a solid return. It can all be done in your attorney's office.

Financing can sometimes be a problem on a split fee, but generally not. Mortgage companies will loan on the building with a subordinated lease, and banks will loan on the land secured by the long-term lease.

In the interest of making a tax-free exchange someday, make the lease for more than thirty years. This allows the lessee of the land and owner of the building to exchange tax free until his lease runs below thirty years.

Example

A shopping center that included five acres of land and several smaller buildings was on the market for sale or exchange. Its evaluation was based mainly on the location of the land and its high traffic count, yet it had not attracted any national leases. The land value was extremely high, better than 80 percent of the total value at the time it was offered. The broker was unable to interest any one party in it, due somewhat to the total cost and the fact that it was an eater until further developed. By splitting the fee, he was able to sell the land to an investment group interested in long-term appreciation and nonmanagement income. He sold the buildings with a 50-year lease on the land to a contractor. The contractor's high income and his building skills were both used to advantage; both his income tax and his tax bracket were lowered because of the heavy depreciation on the present buildings and the availability of heavier depreciation on any new buildings he constructed and leased. By splitting the fee he had financed a pair of transactions unavailable to him before.

11

Trade One Set of Benefits for Another by Exchanging Instead of Buying

You want something you don't have. Isn't that always the case? It is a Mercedes 450SL, or a 40 foot Columbia sailboat, or a new house, or a real estate investment. The problem is that you don't have the ready cash. You have the net worth. You have the wherewithal to make the payment. But you don't have the up front cash to get into the transaction.

What you need to remember is that most people do not have large amounts of cash. Cash is most often used in day-to-day transactions and is not saved for large ones. The key is to use something that has a cash value to get into something you want.

Know How Item

When you have found something you want, offer something that you own other than money. Offer real estate. A whole world of people out there specialize in exchanging real estate instead of buying and selling. The same is true for most big ticket items. Especially in times of tight money. Dealers want out of flooring loans on cars, boats, motorhomes, airplanes. Builders want out of construction loans on homes, duplexes, fourplexes, apartments and condominiums.

Don't be bashful to offer something you no longer have any use for, for something you do have a use for. What's the worst that can happen? He'll say no. But he might say "maybe," or "yes," or "let's see if we can work something out."

Any real estate can be used, no matter where it is. Any personal property can be used. This might be cars, jewelry, paper, stocks and bonds, chits (chits are prepaid meals or lodging or guided hunting trips or airplane rides, etc.). Anything that has value can be used in the right circumstances.

Example

We had some horses out on a 50-acre piece of property in the country and it was becoming a hassle to get out there once a day to feed them and ride them. We had decided that horses were becoming a big part of our lives and that we should either build on the land or find someplace that was built to take horses and people with less effort then we were expending.

My wife searched the real estate columns and found an ideal place. We looked at it. It had everything you could ask for. The owner was asking for a large cash down payment, reasonable monthly payments, and a short-term payoff. We balked. We did not have enough money put aside for such a property, but we liked it very much and we thought about it.

Finally we decided that if we wanted the property as much as we thought we did, we ought at least to make an offer that we could live with. So we did. We offered our house equity subject to a loan; we offered some existing notes and first mortgages that we were holding; and we offered to take a new first mortgage on the "horse" place to get the owner some cash

We felt that we had given the deal our best shot and that surely he would reject the offer. He did not. He said "maybe." After he had examined what we were offering, he agreed. We had gotten what we wanted by making an exchange offer when what he asked for was cash. Our efforts were well rewarded. This is not an isolated example. The truth of the matter is that exchanging works very well. It simply means that you trade one set of benefits for another. The only time people really need cash for their real estate is if they are leaving the real estate field. If they simply wish to move their equity to other properties for different benefits, an exchange will often suit them better than a sale and repurchase of other real estate.

12

How to Get the Twin Benefits of Tax Shelter and Spendable Income Through an Overtrade and Cashback

An investor with large holdings in raw land would like to get out of the payments for awhile and could also use some tax shelter. If he could find a way to convert some of his large equities into tax sheltered properties and at the same time find some spendable income for himself, he would be truly happy.

Know How Item

This can be accomplished by overtrading. You take his large equity and exchange it into someone else's small equity. To balance the difference, you get a note and trust deed on his property, which gives him spendable income.

Example

I was general partner of a syndication which had a huge inventory of building lots and an eightplex apartment house. Lots were not selling well. Most of the apartment houses in town had 20 to 30 percent vacancy. There were many apartment owners who were willing to exchange out so that they could know the exact amount they would have to "put in" each month.

We offered to exchange $300,000 equity in our lots and the eightplex for a $150,000 equity in a twenty-four-unit apartment building. In addition, the owner agreed to give us back a $150,000 note and trust deed on the lots payable in quarterly payments.

Of course, we had the problem of renting the vacant apartments. He had the problem of meeting the payments on the land loans and our new note and trust deed. Fortunately, both the apartment house market and the lot market came back at the same time, so we both got well.

13

How to Exchange and Borrow to Get Your Assets Working for You

These circumstances are somewhat unique. You don't find them every day (although they exist every day). Able owns some free-and-clear lots in an area that is not moving fast. The lots have been on the market for two years with no offers. Able wants cash, but he cannot borrow on the lots. There is no current market for them, and Able is left sitting with an asset that isn't working for him.

Baker is flush with money but has a "user" property that he has been vainly trying to sell. He owns a café, or small motel, or business that requires a Mom and Pop type operation to be successful. The property has little or no financing on it and probably wouldn't qualify for financing from a regular lender in today's market.

Know How Item

Able offers to exchange his free-and-clear lots to Baker for his "user" property, at the same time requesting a loan back on the "user" property. Able gets out of the lots and into the "user property and acquires a good loan on it from Baker. Baker gets the free-and-clear lots, gets rid of his "user" property, and makes a good first loan at a good interest rate, getting some of his cash to work at higher yields.

Example

A corporation owned some free-and-clear lots in a huge subdivision that had originally sold some 1,500 lots, mostly to speculators. The original sale had been made in the hope that many people would move to that area and live in the country while commuting to the city to work. The 1974 gas shortage ended that hope, and the lots were still in the hands of speculators, with very few homes having been built. The lots were going nowhere and besides that, they were in competition with 1,400 other lots. No local lenders would loan on them, and the corporation needed money.

A wealthy passive investor owned a lot of property and was in the midst of converting his "user" properties into passive management properties. At the time, he was also buying commercial paper with banks to get a higher yield on his savings account, which was large. He had an eightplex and a smaller trailer court, neither of which was large enough to attract good management. The free-and-clear lots appealed to him because they required no management.

The corporation offered the lots to him for his equity in the eightplex and the trailer court, provided that he would make the corporation a new first mortgage on the two properties and thereby provide some cash for the company. He did, they did, and it closed with the corporation getting the two "user" properties and a loan they would never have gotten from a lender. Both parties were satisfied and got what they wanted.

14

How to Have Your Cake and Eat It Later

An investor or owner wants to sell or exchange his property, but he is not sure of what he wants to do with the cash he would receive, or what other investment property he might want. What he does know is that he wants "out" of what he has. It could be a hotel, motel, resort, or some high-intensive management property and business, or he could be losing money in a raw land deal or half-vacant apartment house. Since he is unsure of his future, he is reluctant to pay the taxes that are associated with selling or exchanging improperly. He wants out, is hesitant about the taxes that could be levied, and he doesn't know where he wants to go from that point.

Know How Item

By following certain guidelines you can arrange a sale or an exchange that has the look of being taxable, but will permit the investor to get out of the property, have the cash from a sale held for him, or the other person's property held for him. He can then ultimately decide what he wants to do with these assets and have them used in his behalf—without being taxed.

Example

An investor by the name of Alderson wanted a tax-free exchange but was being offered cash from Allied Die Casting Co. Alderson added an amendment to the escrow wherein Alderson would exchange for property Allied Die Casting would buy for him (Allied Die Casting Co.—Aldersons—Appellate Court 1957 V. 317 Fed. 2nd P. 790).

There were five actions that the judge said made it tax-free.

1. The exchange provided for an alternate cash sale. It was clear what they would do and did do.
2. Taxpayer may require purchaser to use his cash to improve, purchase other property, or anything prior to close of escrow.
3. Alderson looked at the property he ultimately got and negotiated for it.
4. A sale was provided for in the event the exchange failed. Judge said ok to that.
5. The taxpayer's contractual relationship was limited to the other party in the exchange.

The three rings that must not happen in order for a transaction to be tax-free are:

1. Taxpayer who is claiming a tax-deferred exchange cannot receive any purchase cash.

2. The taxpayer cannot receive any cash through an agent acting for him.
3. People involved in the transactions must deal at arm's length and it must be clear what they did.

In the event of a sale, the taxpayer cannot have constructive receipt of the money. It must be held where he cannot benefit from its use during the time he is deciding what to acquire. If it is clear that the sale is for the purpose of acquiring another property that would qualify as a tax-deferred exchange, and if the cash is held by a third party with no access to it by the taxpayer, and if it is documented and clearly followed through, the cash can be used to acquire another property and avoid tax, providing the property acquired qualifies.

15

Creation of Paper: How to Put a Frozen Equity to Work in a Tight Money Market

Creation of paper is probably the least understood financing technique. By paper, I mean an equity committed in writing, such as a mortgage or trust deed. It is so simple to do that most people find it hard to believe that it works. Once understood and used, however, it can become a valid and valuable tool in releasing equities to exchange or buy property.

Writing the instrument is an attorney's job, but you can work it up with your client so that it fits his ability to repay. That is the easy part about creating paper. To illustrate, let's assume you have a client with a free-and-clear property with a fair market value of $100,000. It is an income-producing property and can stand a good mortgage of at least $70,000. But in creating paper you do not use a mortgage company. You do not pay points for the money or suffer under tight money regulations. Instead, you tailor-make the paper to your client's abilities to repay.

With the $100,000 free-and-clear property you create a first mortgage or trust deed for $40,000 with low payments and low interest and use that to secure a property your client wants to fit his portfolio. Then you create a second for $20,000 the same way and use that to exchange for another equity.

Know How Item

In a tight money market, or in order to save loan costs, create paper on good solid equities to move your client's frozen money into the market again. The creation of paper has two distinct advantages:

1. The amount of the created paper is added to the encumbrance of the property for your new book basis on the property you acquire.
2. You can tailor-make the paper to fit any situation with any payback that is feasible. You are not bound by normal mortgage lending problems.

Example

A psychologist client of mine decided to run for political office, and, feeling certain that he would win, decided to set up an income property that would provide him with spendable income when he chose to retire from the field of political combat some ten years hence. We discussed it often and finally decided to use some free-and-clear land that bordered the river, a part of his "farm" not included in the new mortgage just placed on his house and four acres. The land had a solid value of $60,000 according to recent sales in the area, so we decided to create a first mortgage against the property in the amount of $12,000 payable over five years at 10 percent interest with annual payments which best suited his income picture. It is extremely difficult to borrow money on bare land in our area for less than 15 percent unless it is working, producing land. Idle land waiting for development has little mortgage value.

Creation of Paper: How to Put a Frozen Equity to Work

We used that paper to exchange on an apartment house, which would eventually solve the retirement problem by supplying some $600 spendable income per month. I took the created paper for my free and was able to borrow the full amount from the doctor's banker.

By the way, when you create wealth for a client he pays a brokerage fee on the paper as if it were property.

16

How to Buy, Option, Sell, and Exchange Paper

The business of real estate paper can be a full-time job. Real estate paper exists everywhere. There are good times and bad times for this paper and its various owners. Generally, it is a bad time to buy when there is a "boom" on and people want to cash out by getting new financing. Even then, however, there are properties that do not lend themselves to cash out sales—properties that need owner financing, the sale of which produces "paper."

Generally, it is a good time to buy paper when financing costs are high and there is a downturn in the economy, forcing sellers who must sell to take back paper on the sale of their property.

Let's examine the terms used here to better convey what happens when paper develops.

> **Paper:** any note and trust deed, mortgage, or contract that has real estate as security for payment of the note.

Discount: the amount of money that is taken off the face value of the paper to entice a buyer to buy that paper.

Yield: the percentage return per year that can be expected from the capital required to purchase any paper if it pays out as per the terms of the note.

Bonus-yield: the percentage return that is "speculated" on due to probability of an early payoff of the existing paper, thereby shortening the payback time and increasing the yield.

Since many sellers of real estate must help finance the sale of their property by carrying back paper, and since many sellers either need or want cash, their paper creates a supply.

The demand portion of this functioning market is met by the people who have cash and want the higher yields of real estate paper.

The two are brought together by a fluctuating yield on this paper that goes up or down depending on amount of money available; yields on government securities; the prime rate; savings account rates; and the general feeling of the economy. When the holder of paper is willing to sell to the buyer of paper at a yield that induces the buyer to buy, we have a market. I have seen many times when the two could not come together often enough to call it a market. A few desperate sellers would sell, but not enough to call it a market.

The buyers want a "yield" high enough to make them want to invest their cash in a piece of paper. In the last twenty years this has fluctuated from a low of 9 percent to a high of 35 percent. This means the annual rate of return on their invested dollar. If a note has a face value of $10,000 and it is being paid back at the rate of $100 per month which includes interest at 10 percent, the $10,000 is yielding 10 percent.

To get the yield up from the 10 percent interest, buyers offer to buy paper at a discount. They discount the face amount of the paper so that they pay less than the face amount, thereby increasing their yield on the smaller amount of cash invested. Say they pay $8,000 for the $10,000 note and still get the $100 per month and 10 percent on the $10,000. The $2,000 difference between the face amount of the note ($10,000) and the price they paid for it ($8,000) is the discount. To determine the yield, you must look in a table or work it out on a calculator. But in our example, the yield has jumped from 10 percent to 13.71 percent by discounting the face amount $2,000.

Another factor now comes into play: When the buyer of the paper discounts the face amount, he is counting on the payor of the paper to make all his payments until the note is paid in full. What if the payor pays out early? He refinances the property, or sells it. What happens to the investor's yield? IT GOES UP . . . and fast!

Assume that the payor of the $10,000 note makes his monthly payments of $100 for a year, then pays off the balance of the note. The investor has not only received $1,200 in payments that year, but has earned the $2,000 difference between the $8,000 he paid for the note and the $10,000 repaid. His overall return is about $3,000 on the $8,000 note, or a 35 percent yield for that year. (Twelve payments of $100 equals $1,200, minus $200 to principal, leaving approximately $1,000 in interest, plus the $2,000 discounted, equals a total of $3,000 in round figures.)

Setting Up to Buy It

It is not that difficult to do. You can do it big or small, slow or fast. Determine how much money you are going to use. Establish your criteria for purchase of the paper which should include the following:

Locale: are you going to buy anywhere or just in your town?

Price: what market are you going to be in—$5,000 or $500,000?

Position: are you going to buy only first paper, or seconds and thirds?

Amount of capital to any one paper: would you invest as much as 50 percent of your capital in one paper? What if it goes bad?

Liquidity: are you going to keep a portion of your capital readily available at all times—or spent up to the wall?

To purchase a paper you can use an attorney, an escrow, or do it yourself. If you are unknowledgeable, or busy, I suggest that you use an escrow officer for closing and an attorney to draw the legal documents.

You can option paper. You may be expecting some cash within thirty days and want a particular paper but can't buy it now. Or you wish to sell it to someone else and make a profit. Use the option.

You can hold the paper. After all, if you own something that is yielding 10 to 35 percent a year, and you need the cash flow, that is hard to beat. To hold it you need to have a simple system. This system is merely to let you record the payments and date of payments, the amount paid on interest and principal, and the outstanding balance.

I keep two files. One file is for the bookkeeping department and records the monthly payment information. This allows bookkeeping to inform me of the profit and loss on a monthly basis. The second file is the information file. It has a copy of all documents in it, names, addresses and phone numbers of the people involved; where they work, credit reports, references—in other words everything that I have on the property and the people. This is only referred to in case of litigation or in circumstances where the paper does not work out according to the terms and conditions of the note and trust deed.

How to Sell Paper

If you want to get into selling paper you need several things. You may need a securities license in your state. Many states view buying and selling paper in any volume to be a securities business in that you are selling a partial interest in real estate instead of the fee simple. You will need a group of buyers. There are two ways you can sell paper.

1. You can sell the paper to them at less than you paid for it and make a profit, while they own it and take care of it.
2. You can find the paper for them, sell it to them for more than you paid for it, guarantee, collect, and bank it for them.

There are benefits to each system and you will have to decide which suits you best.

The people to look for in building a following of buyers are people who want and need higher returns on their money: military officers, elderly people on fixed incomes, pension trusts, retirees, and other people who have some residual cash that they can invest without high tax consequences from the cash flow generated. The income from paper is basically all ordinary income—mostly interest, and while you can occasionally get some capital gain income from paper activities, you are mostly in the ordinary income tax bracket.

Pension trust funds and profit sharing plans are good prospects for purchase of paper. Getting to know their investment officers can provide you with ready source of cash for purchase.

How to Exchange Paper

Once you have acquired some paper you do not need to just hold on to it, or to sell it to another party. You can also exchange it. You may have bought the paper for sixty cents on the dollar. You can probably exchange it for one hundred cents on the dollar. What you need to look for is someone in a set of circumstances that promotes his desire to own passive paper and get out of whatever he is in. I have exchanged paper for cars, land, vacation lots, apartment houses, my personal homes, airplanes, furs, jewelry, time in Hawaiian condominiums, horses, instruction in flying; also for real estate classes, clothes, tailoring, carpentry, office rent, guided hunts, and boats.

Many people would be willing to take paper at face value if only they were asked. If they have something on the market that you want and you can offer them paper at face value that you paid less for, *ASK THEM TO TAKE IT!* I know several brokers who pay their rent with paper at face value that they acquired at a discount.

Tax Consequences of Dealing in Paper

Buying and holding paper produces tax consequences depending on how much volume you do. If it is an occasional transaction, you will probably be taxed at ordinary income rates on the interest earned. Perhaps you will also have to pay a capital gains tax on the difference between the face value you ultimately receive and the price you paid for it. If you do any great volume, most probably that will be wiped out and it will all be income earned in the course of your business—buying and holding paper.

If you are buying and selling you complicate the matter a bit more. The paper you hold will be treated one way, the paper you sell, another. If you get this deeply involved, you will probably be called a dealer in paper and it will all be ordinary income anyway.

Optioning and buying will most likely produce the same tax treatment, since your options will not generally extend over a year, thus keeping you in the short-term capital gain tax rate which is the same as the ordinary income tax rate.

Exchanging is more difficult to follow. If you own paper and exchange it at a profit, that profit may go untaxed and simply lower your basis in the property you acquire with the paper. On the other hand it could trigger taxation on the paper profit based on the fair market value of the property you acquire. It is always best to review any event with your tax advisor prior to entering into negotiations, so you have a good idea of what you can do without triggering a taxable event. If you exchange the paper at your basis (cost less amounts received) for some real estate you most probably would not need to report it as income.

How to Buy Paper at Wholesale and Exchange it at Retail

First set your goals. It is always best to know why you are entering into an endeavor, and that is determined by asking yourself why you are going to do this. What do you hope to attain by doing so? And how long do you intend to do it? With these goals in mind, you can now flesh out the program.

Your goals might be to turn $10,000 into $100,000 in paper or property within a five-year time frame. To be cautious, honorable, honest, and tough but fair. Starting with the $10,000 you will need to set up goals as mentioned earlier in this chapter about locale, price, position, liquidity, etc.

Now put an ad in the newspaper. Say you will buy notes and deeds of trust or mortgages or contracts, and include your phone number. You might also mail letters to all real estate offices or licensees, escrow officers, bank loan officers, lawyers, accountants—all of whom come in contact with sellers of paper. Very soon, you will become known to these people, and you should have a great deal of paper presented to you.

Buy it right. Try to let your business mind control the price you offer for a paper. Usually the buyer sets up the criteria that must be present before he will entertain an offer to buy paper. This will weed out many sellers of paper. Quickly run through your basic criteria when you preview a piece of paper. If it meets your first standards, then take more time to review it thoroughly.

Proceeding to your goals you buy the paper. Let's say you have been able to purchase $15,000 worth of paper for $10,000 cash. Now following the yellow brick road becomes interesting. There are several paths you can take. One I might suggest is that you exchange that $15,000 piece of paper for a free-and-clear $15,000 house; get a new loan on it for $10,000 thus replacing your original capital; rent the house to make the payments; and start looking for more paper with the $10,000. While you are buying more paper, the house is appreciating, the debt is being reduced, and you are getting tax credits on depreciation and interest paid.

If you don't have $15,000 houses in your area, buy in an area that does, or get more paper together, or get a free-and-clear lot. Then, get a loan on that or sell it and get more paper. As you can see, it goes on and on and on and on.

If you have a continuing source of funds so that you do not need to replenish them from maneuverings with the paper you have already acquired, you might consider exchanging the paper on property that will appreciate or produce taxable losses or both.

Only twice in more than twenty years in the real estate business have I had people want to discount my paper when it was offered in an exchange. Both of those have been in Alaska and in the last year.

You can build an estate by buying paper at a discount and exchanging it for investment real estate. Lots, rental houses, duplexes, fourplexes, small office buildings, and apartment houses—all can be acquired using paper at face-value. Maybe not for the whole amount, but coupled with some cash and some refinancing or owner financing, you can acquire with face value paper for which you paid considerably less. As you get more paper and more money you can play different games with more variety, such as selling one paper to get the cash you need to sweeten the paper you are offering at face-value on an investment property.

Paper Can Be Fun and Games Or a Money-Making Hobby

It does not take much time or money or aptitude to buy paper. You can hire the talent to make sure the purchase is correct and draw the documents and even collect the payments through an escrow. The only problem is if the paper doesn't pay and you have to foreclose. That can present a problem. But if you stick to first trust deeds or mortgages, you are generally in pretty good shape if the security has been kept up and not allowed to deteriorate.

From that standpoint, paper makes a good hobby for people without much else to do. You can buy, hold, and from the monthly

How to Buy, Option, Sell and Exchange Paper

payments build up your nest egg to buy again—and from the payoff of one paper along with more monthly payments buy another paper. Over and over it rolls, making you more wealthy with each turn.

Yields on paper are fun to watch. Let's take our example of a note and trust deed with a face value of $10,000, paying $100 per month including principal and interest at 10 percent. If you were to buy that at the various prices below your yield would differ:

Face Amount	Price Paid	Annual Yield
$10,000	$9,000	11.69
10,000	8,000	13.71
10,000	7,000	16.19
10,000	6,000	19.37
10,000	5,000	23.64

Now assume that instead of just paying out at $100 per month until date of maturity, there is a balloon payment of the balance due in five years. How does that change the yield?

Face Amount	Price Paid	Annual Yield
$10,000	$9,000	12
10,000	8,000	15
10,000	7,000	17
10,000	6,000	20
10,000	5,000	25

17

How Exchanging Paper Can Generate a Steady Cash Flow

You have some real estate paper. Maybe you sold your house, or lot, business property, or investment, and you carried back some of the debt. The buyer of the property owes you some money and he is paying it off by the month, by the year, or by some method that finally pays off the note and mortgage or trust deed or contract.

Maybe you bought it. There are active buyers and sellers of real estate paper in the market.

Either way you are the holder, the beneficiary, of some real estate paper that is paying something per month, at a rate of interest that is reasonable, with a due date on the debt sometime in the future. It can be a first or second or third mortgage or trust deed. The point of this technique is that you own it and apparently have only two alternatives open to you:

1. Hold it and collect the payments as they come in. Meanwhile the balance is shrinking all the time and inflation is eating up the buying power of the payments and remaining principal balance.
2. Sell that paper on the open market to a buyer who wants to discount the face value of it so that he can get a higher yield. His demands for yield are normally close to two times the prime rate.

You may think you have only two alternatives, but it's not so. You have another choice. You can exchange that paper and acquire all kinds of benefits.

Know How Item

There are four main benefits to investing in real estate. They are:

1. Cash flow,
2. Principal reduction,
3. Tax shelter,
4. Appreciation.

After deciding that holding the paper for the payments or selling it at a discount do not suit your investment goals then consider this: You can exchange that paper.

The key to exchanging it is to find someone who wants the benefits the paper provides. Real estate paper provides several benefits. One is cash flow. The money that comes in each month provides a generally consistent supply of cash. It consists of principal and interest, so the debt goes down each month which eventually means you have nothing at the end. In other words, paper does not appreciate. It provides no tax shelter. It provides no principal reduction. However, it requires no management to get the cash flow.

Different people hold paper for different reasons. The people to search out are elderly people who want continued cash flow for a limited number of years. Often, these people have a house that they have lived in for years, want to move to a different location and like to have paper to pay them a steady income. We often guarantee the paper we exchange to elderly people to give them the added assurance that if the paper goes into default, we will step in and buy it back on the same terms or replace it with another paper to their liking. This removes their fear of having to come back and foreclose when they have moved and know very little about paper.

Example

I was attempting to raise some cash and decided to use some accumulated real estate notes and mortgages to do so. I approached the discounters and found that market conditions would cause me to lose $18,000 on some $50,000 in paper, netting me only $32,000 in cash. It seemed a bit harsh at the time, so I began looking for a free-and-clear house that someone had held for a long time—someone who could benefit from holding the paper and would accept it at face value.

An elderly couple about to retire had a house that they had outgrown. Because the house had been added on to and changed around here and there to fit their family as they had grown, it was not a red hot seller on the current market.

They wanted to move to Arizona. Their retirement income and the paper income would do them well. I made the offer and it was accepted. I offered them the $50,000 paper for their $50,000 house free-and-clear. I was able to mortgage the house for $40,000 (which was $8,000 more than the discounters would have paid me for the paper) and I still owned the equity of $10,000. I rented the house to make the mortgage payment for several years, then sold it for $57,500.

I still hear occasionally from the widow of the couple. He died a year ago and she is still receiving some of the paper income, which has been most helpful to her.

18

How to Buy a Property for 20 Percent Off While Seller Gets His Asking Price

Able has a property for sale and you want it. He is willing to sell and take back paper—in other words, to help finance the transaction by agreeing to carry part of his equity back in the form of a note and trust deed (mortgage) to himself. You have enough cash to cash him out, or you can get enough through financing his property and using the cash you have.

You can get that property for a considerable discount if you will employ the following technique. It will not always work, but it will work often enough to make a believer of you. There is also a twist that will allow you to buy the property and actually put money back in your pocket.

Know How Item

You negotiate the transaction with the seller, including how much cash it will take, how much paper, at what interest rate, and for how long. Insert into the transaction wording along these lines: "Seller agrees to accept paper on property other than what he is selling herein, providing that it is on acceptable property, and similar terms, conditions, and position." Or, "Purchaser may substitute other paper on property not included in this transaction for the paper seller is agreeing to carry back on his property, providing however, that seller approves of the property that is security for the paper; the terms, conditions, and position of the paper are similar to that seller is taking. Seller may not unreasonably withhold consent for replacement of paper."

These phrases help clarify your position after you have discussed it with the seller. Now your problem is to find some paper that you can buy at a discount using the rest of the cash you had. Your goal is to purchase a piece of paper at a discount that your seller will accept in place of his carryback on the property that he is selling you.

If you don't know anyone who buys and sells paper, look in your newspaper. There is generally a heading "WANTED TO BUY" or "WANT TO SELL." From the buyers you can often get a piece of paper that will meet your needs. From the sellers you will find paper that you will need to scrutinize. If you don't know anything about paper, get in touch with someone who does—a real estate broker, banker, or lawyer. Get someone who has dealt in it, not someone who has only a superficial knowledge of it.

When you find a suitable paper, make an offer to purchase that will give you a yield of close to twice the current prime rate. There are many different formulas for buying and selling paper. Second and third trust deeds almost always sell for less than firsts. The higher the interest rate, the shorter the payoff, the larger the monthly payments, the more you will have to pay for the paper in relation to its face value, but the yield could be the same.

Option the paper first until you get your seller to accept it in lieu of his. Then consummate the purchase of the paper and put it into the transaction at the closing of escrow.

Example

A young realtor friend of mine was spending much of his time learning by doing. His latest crusade was to find a situation where he could apply this technique. He found it. The owner of an eightplex was willing to accept "soft" paper* on other property, and some cash for his property. He came to me seeking to find some existing paper that he could purchase at a discount. I didn't have any, but suggested that we make an offer to exchange that would include some cash and other paper.

Together we structured an offer that included some free-and-clear lots at appraised value; some paper paying interest of 10 percent or more, interest only with no due date; and some cash.

Our next job was to get it accepted. It was. Now we had to find some existing paper paying at least 10 percent interest that was in a first or second position and on acceptable property.

We found a subdivider who had a lot of paper paying from 9 percent to 14 percent interest—all seconds after a land improvement loan with a local bank, and all due on first construction draw or five years, whichever was first. Land had been very slow for the last two years and he was hurting. We offered to buy $150,000 face value of the paper for $90,000 cash providing our eightplex seller would accept the paper.

The eightplex owner accepted the paper and we closed the purchase of the paper at the same time we closed the purchase of the eightplex. For the $300,000 eightplex we had given $75,000 in cash; $150,000 in paper; and $75,000 in free-and-clear lots. By paying only $90,000 for the $150,000 in paper we had saved $60,000, which was 20 percent of the purchase price.

The Twist

You exchange cash and paper that you buy at a discount for a free-and-clear property. You can frequently borrow more on the property from a lender than you paid out in cash for the paper and the down payment. This twist allows you to buy the property—and it puts extra cash in your pocket.

---

*Soft paper: a term used to describe paper with lower than market interest rate; long-term payment; and maybe a substitution clause, thereby differentiating it from "hard paper" which is high interest; large payments; and short payoff period.

19

How to Use the Broker's Fee in Financing the Transaction

In a sale, transaction money is available from four sources:

1. The seller's equity;
2. The buyer's down payment;
3. The reserves and closing costs;
4. The broker's fee.

You may disagree with item number 3 on the grounds that reserves belong to the seller and closing costs must be paid. However, there have been many transactions that closed because the seller left in the reserves or took back a note for them, and escrow and title companies have often waited for their charges.

The broker's fee, and along with it the salesman's fee, usually amount to from 5 to 10 percent of the total price. This is as much as most down payments and can often make the transaction where other financing is not available. I am not suggesting that you leave all fees to the financing. Many of my friends and I have made the mistake of committing too many fees to paper and have jeopardized our cash position. You must decide for yourself, and generally with each transaction, whether you are in a position to accept paper for your fee.

You can accept paper for every fee and be perfectly liquid if you follow prudent money management and consult often with the bank and private parties who buy or lend on secured paper. Let's assume you have agreed to take paper for your fee and it is to be secured by a mortgage on a parcel of real estate. If it is a first encumbrance, pays above 6 percent interest, and has regular monthly payments of reasonable size, you will have no problem borrowing on the paper or selling it.

If you sell it to a private party, you can most likely expect a discount of 10 to 50 percent, depending on the quality of the paper, the security, and the people who are behind the paper. After you have taken a few and sold a few, you will learn how to check these things out. But if you wish to learn the easy way, read on.

A paper with a good rate of interest, usually 10 percent and above, with good security, hopefully a first mortgage or trust deed, payable monthly over not more than three to five years, and signed by people with a good credit rating will take the least discount—probably not more than 20 percent. The theory behind the discount is that with money in your hand now, you have prevented loss by inflation (roughly 6 percent a year) and you have the money to put back to work at once. You also eliminate the possible risk and problem of foreclosure on the property to save your loan.

Many brokers simply refuse to become involved in the lending business and, make no mistake, that *is* what you are doing. You are lending your fee to one of the parties and you should follow prudent business practices when lending money. But to brokers who follow sound practices, will not settle all fees in paper, and are willing to take certain risks, there is a wealth of opportunity to build an estate with fees they would otherwise have refused.

I have seen many salesmen eager to get a transaction signed agree to take paper without thinking of the consequences. Remember, however, that if you have to discount it to sell it you have not received a full fee. Most real estate fees in paper are around 10 percent, and that is tough to sell without a large discount. The banks will lend you money on a good note up to the amount that the note will pay the first two years, but they will discount it to yield them current interest rates.

If you can hold it and do not need the cash, you earn interest and it should be in the range of 10 percent to 20 percent. The banks charge that much simple interest on a note. Now if you decide you can afford to keep the note and earn the interest on your fee, you have still another problem. If you have it well secured and the payments are definite and inescapable for the party who owes it to you, you have created a tax problem. You must include the fair market value of that note in your income for the year in which you receive it and pay income taxes on it. If, in the eyes of the IRS, it is 100 percent secure, you are paying tax on income you have not yet received. Now, take it to three people who buy notes and ask them to bid on it. The highest of the three bids you write on the back of the note: (U.S. Bank will buy for $2,000 May 12, 1981). You thank them and return it to your portfolio. A $6,000 note then, will sell today for $2,000, and you pay income tax on that amount.

You pay tax on the balance of the note as you receive it—UNLESS you take my next suggestion. Read on.

Let's say you have accumulated $20,000 worth of fee paper at 12 percent interest that pays out over five years. You have taken it to your bank and have had a fair market value placed on it of $12,000. You will pay tax on that $12,000 this year if you keep it. If you trade it for property, you will pay tax on it at the *value you trade it for*. BUT—you can receive enough depreciation from the improved real estate in most instances to offset the tax you would have paid for it.

Taking paper for a fee is like taking whiskey for a cough. If it helps, do it. If it is to your advantage to borrow on it or sell it, to hold it and earn interest, or to exchange it on other property, then do it. Some brokers with annual incomes over $100,000 take most of their fees in paper spread over several years to avoid tax on large portions in one year. Others with a single large income in one year will average their income as allowed by the IRS.

I have taken accumulated paper fees many times and exchanged them at face value for a free-and-clear house and then mortgaged the house to pick up cash. I either added the houses to my portfolio and rented them, or listed them with another broker and sold them. Several times I have mortgaged such a house and exchanged the remaining equity to a party I owed paper to, so it works itself around after awhile.

Know How Item

Paper has value. Take it for fees that you would not otherwise have if you insisted on cash. Write it for high interest, short term, and get as good security as possible. Then do with it what best fits your situation. Borrow on it or sell it. Keep it and earn interest. Exchange it on real estate to create cash and an equity. Exchange it on investment property that will build your estate.

20

Financing Financed Raw Land: How to Get Out of "Eat" and Maintain Appreciation

The day of no surprises is past. As the economic market changes rapidly, we have come to find that once unusual circumstances are now relatively common. One of these not-so-unusual situations involves a builder or developer who bought some land for future use, but due to tight money discovers that getting a construction loan is now out of the question. Often, due to the scarcity of construction money, the market for this encumbered land has softened so much that the value has dipped below the amount owed on the land. The builder can't hold on, and he can't sell below his loans. He also knows that he will have a good, legitimate equity when the upswing comes around. His goal is to get out of the "negative" cash flow position that has him in a bind, but to retain some of the equity when the upturn in the economy finally comes.

Know How Item

If you are sure the property will appreciate, and if it is highly usable in a different market which you feel is coming, then get an investor with a high cash flow to come in and carry the payments while the builder's equity sits there. Give the investor some percentage of the equity (usually 50 percent) in return for his carrying the payments until the land is developed. When the land is developed, the investor might also lend his financial statement to the project to acquire a better loan

Benefits

Both the builder and the investor benefit from this arrangement. The builder gets to keep the growth land even though the market is temporarily soft, and he can develop it when money becomes more available and the need is there. Also, he does not lose whatever equity he had in the property by foreclosure, and he gets rid of the payments that were bothering him. The investor gets in on the "old" value, generally at a lower interest rate than current purchases, and he does it without having to put in a down payment. He simply has to make the payments and taxes when due to pick up 50 percent of something sometime later down the road. He also now has a knowledgeable partner.

Example

A client of mine had bought some very good commercial land on a beautiful contract that allowed for interest only payments for four years, starting with 4 percent and ending at 8 percent. It would then begin to amortize at a pretty stiff figure. My client planned on having it developed by that time, and he figured that the income would take care of the steeper payments. His plans did not work and he found himself faced with the stiff payments before the income stream was well developed. In a blaze of genius, he bought in an investor who had a heavy cash flow from his business. My client gave him 50 percent of the equity if he would make the payments and pay all expenses until the property was developed enough to support itself. The arrangement worked well. The project was eventually completed, and the last parcel netted them more cash than they originally paid for the entire parcel.

Good Use

If you are exchanging into something where you hesitate to take over the large payments but will have a good equity if you can make the transaction, get an investor with a heavy cash flow to come in and make all the payments (and/or expenses) and get 50 percent (or some portion) of the equity for his financial contribution. Of course, the goal must be to make the property self-sufficient or sell it before the investor has more than equaled your original equity.

21

Payments Don't Always Include Principal and Interest—and Sometimes Not Even Interest

---

There are two situations to which this technique is readily applicable—and probably hundreds more unresearched.

Situation one: An investor is saddled with a building that is not sufficiently occupied to make its payments and expenses. He is dying to sell it. It is listed with the normal down payment and monthly payments. But an analysis of the operating statements clearly reveals that anyone else buying the building will have to fork out a ton of money to keep the property alive until it fills up, which is expected to take two years.

Situation two: A small partnership owns some commercially zoned land on a frontage road. They have it listed for sale, along with every other parcel along that road. The appraisals have increased in value over the last three years but no one has bought and built anything—so far it's just speculators betting on the outcome. The partners are tired of making payments and want out.

Know How Item

Make an offer wherein the total payments made are not enough to cover principal and interest—in fact not enough to cover even the interest payments. It will work if the seller has enough equity so that the payments you make to him are sufficient to handle his underlying debt payments.

Here's how it works. Simply offer an amount monthly or quarterly or annually that you or your group feels comfortable with and that relieves you of having to come up with huge amounts of cash to cover the seller's equity payments. Simply take the amount of the payment you are willing to make and apply it to the interest due. Since it will not pay it all, the balance is carried over to the next month and it continues to add up.

A variation on this is to make a down payment with no payment at all for some period, say two years. Let the interest owed add on during that time and when payments start again, they first apply to the interest.

Example

A syndication I had formed to purchase a subdivision needed some early cash to finish installation of utilities and additional monthly payments to help carry the debt on the property. We offered some of the more desirable land for sale. We hoped to attract investors who would snap it up while we continued to develop the inner portions of the subdivision.

An offer came in to us with a smallish down payment and smallish monthly payments. We countered with requests for more money in both departments. They countered with a larger down payment and no payments for two years. After that, they would make good-sized quarterly payments at an interest rate that was above what we were paying. We quickly calculated that at the end of the two years, they would have built up so much interest debt that their quarterly payments would be 99 percent interest. That was what they wanted. Their holding period would be all interest and therefore deductible. We agreed proving they would agree to an eight-year balloon payment. They said ten years and we agreed. It closed.

The Moral? You can often accept payments that don't cover interest if that technique solves a problem.

22

The Many Advantages of Separating the Down Payment From the Principal

There is a psychological advantage from the buyer's standpoint in making an offer that differs from the usual, treating the down payment as a special transaction. Most sellers want a large down payment, and most buyers offer a small down payment. Most sellers want the balance to be paid out in a short period of time or have a balloon to shorten the total time payment if they are asked to carry some of the financing.

Let's say you have an opportunity to purchase an apartment building that is being offered at $2,300,000 with terms of $500,000 down and the balance over ten years. It doesn't make economic sense to pay it off over that period of time, nor to put that much capital down at closing. But it is a good building, good location, and growth potential is good. It has all the makings of the right deal for your operation except for down payment and terms.

Know How Item

Split up the down payment. Offer $200,000 at closing; $150,000 in the next tax year; and $150,000 in the second tax year. This will scatter the down payment over three tax years and allow the property to help make the down payment. You can offer interest on the unpaid principal, often at a reduced rate from the carry-back or underlying mortgage.

You can make the future down-payment portions subject to certain attainments—for instance, reaching projected rent rates or occupancy rates. You can use it when the seller reaches a break-even cash flow, or in conjunction with a lease-back by the seller.

Then, deal separately with the principal balance that will be left *after* the full down payment is received. For instance: The balance on the $2,300,000 purchase *after* the $500,000 down payment is made is $1,800,000. Treat that amount separately, offering payments, interest rate, and ballons suitable to the market on that portion alone, without referring to the down payment.

The seller will adjust psychologically and move with you on those points. He will understand the down payment and treat that separately from the balance on the principal.

Example

We listed a fifty-unit apartment house for $2,300,000. We asked for $500,000 down and the balance at 11 percent interest over twenty-five years. The seller owed about $1,400,000 at 10.25 percent over twenty-four years.

A prospective purchaser was found by another agent who offered the full asking price but split the down payment into three portions: $200,000 at closing, which was in December; $150,000 to be paid eight months later in the next tax year; and the remaining $150,000 to be paid twelve months after the second payment. Interest on the remaining unpaid down payment was to be at 10 percent.

The balance of $1,800,000 was to be by overriding deed of trust, interest only at 11 percent, with an all-due-and-payable clause in eight years. It was also to be leased back by the seller for one year to prove his operating expenses were accurate.

Benefits

The benefits to the purchasers were that they acquired a prime property for an initial down payment of 9 percent. They also spread out the down payment over three years, making it easier for their investors to come up with the remaining down payment. They also got tremendous tax benefits during those three years because of the great leverage produced by the down payment initially.

The sellers could look forward to large increments of cash to be infused into their personal finances in three years, and they had a stronger buyer in the bargain. This was probably a stronger deal than would have been consummated with an individual buyer.

23

How to Convert Principal Payments to Tax Deductible Lease Payments

An investor wants to sell a building but has found no buyers. He has a bank that will lend 60 percent to a good buyer at a decent interest rate. A buyer approaches with a solid down payment, but he wants a higher yield than will be obtainable with a standard purchase.

Know How Item

With a willing seller, and a willing buyer, and a bank that understands yields, you can put this one together. The goal is to convert what would have been principal payments on a normal twenty-five-year amortization to lease payments that are deductible.

This solves the problem of large, well-built buildings that have a long life from the depreciation standpoint, but a short-term amortization from a lender's standpoint. With the short amortization period, the principal portion of the loan is disproportionatley high. By converting the taxable principal payments to deductible lease payments, you have the solution.

Example

Able, the seller, wants $1,000,000 for his building. Baker, the buyer, has $400,000 and wants to buy the building. The bank is willing to loan $600,000 at 12 percent interest.

Instead of buying, Baker leases the building for ten years at $103,300 a year from Able. Able sells the lease to the bank. It yields a gross income over the lease period of $1,032,990, for $600,000 cash. The discount serves as the interest factor to the bank. Baker puts in his $400,000.

Benefits

Able wanted $1,000,000 for his building. He got $600,000 from the bank for sale of the lease and $400,000 from the buyer, so he got what he wanted.

The bank was willing to loan $600,000 on the property and now owns the lease worth $1,032,990 which has the interest element built into it.

Baker now has a building that cost him $400,000. He writes off the $103,300 lease payment each year, in effect writing off his substituted principal and interest payment each year until the lease is paid off.

24

How to Acquire Land With No Cash

The land lease is used increasingly by sophisticated developers and syndicates. It serves so many purposes for a developer (and for the owner of the land as well) that it is bound to find more favor as our tax laws become more and more confiscatory on gain.

A lease for over thirty years is exchangeable tax free under federal law. Most land leases for new buildings will be from thirty to ninety-nine years. The owner of the land realizes several advantages. He can lease it for a monthly payment that will bring him more than he would have received through the sale. The land also remains in his estate to pass on to his heirs. With a new building on his property, he has good security, provided the financing is sound. The mortgage reduces every payment and the property increases in value every year, through appreciation. The lessor does not pay capital gains tax as he would on a sale, he keeps title to the land, gets a guaranteed income, and eventually gets the building on it free and clear.

The lessee also has several advantages. He can include the value of the land in the overall value of the project, which the mortgage lender takes into consideration. He does not need to pay for the land, which he cannot depreciate for return of his capital. He can write the lease payments off his income as an expense item, which he could not do if he were paying for it. The only thing the lessee loses is the appreciation value in the increased charges he asks of tenants for the well-located land, building and amenities.

Know How Item

When capital is short, the owner's problems would be better solved without a sale. If the developer wants a lease, try the land lease. Preprinted lease forms are available, but I strongly suggest you sit down with your attorney and draw up a land lease that covers all the legal points needed to protect all parties. There should be room later on for the lessor to increase the payments on the lease due to appreciation, increased land taxes, and inflation. The land lease generally offers something for each party that would be unavailable to them through sale and purchase.

Example

A corporate client of mine needed a parcel of land adjoining theirs, and I was asked to look into it. The gentleman who owned it was not wild about selling. He had a business and several real estate investments that made him a good living, and as his basis in the property was very low, he had no motivation to sell it. He felt it was as good as any other property he might acquire through an exchange and so was not really willing to spend much time talking about it.

When I mentioned a land lease, he became interested. We arranged for the corporation to start paying him on a land lease, while the old buildings were still usable as apartments, on a net-net-net basis, where my clients paid all taxes, assessments, and any costs against the property. The lease ran for ninety-nine years, which took it past the time anybody in the room would be interested in it. It called for subordination to a construction loan, the terms of the loan to be approved by the lessee. It permitted no new financing on the property without the lessee's consent, and it allowed for removal of the present buildings after written commitment had been granted for a new construction loan.

The lessor had an income for ninety-nine years of not less than $100 a month and not a worry in the world. The corporation had the use of the land without sinking any capital into it.

25

How to Get 100 Percent Financing By Sale and Leaseback

Developer Able has a property that he is ready to develop, and he is looking for a high degree of financing. He needs cash to make the project go, and he also needs the work of putting the project together. The conventional lenders are looking for something more than the normal loan and amortization, and in the fluctuating interest market, they are a little uneasy about a long-term normal loan. Each has what the other needs to stay in business.

Know How Item

There are two methods of sale and leaseback that provide a high degree of financing.

1. The land is sold to a lending institution and then leased back by the developer. Then the leasehold interest in the improvements is mortgaged and generally the developer can get 100 percent of the land value in the sale to the lender, and 75 percent of the value of the improvements in the loan.
2. The developer places a maximum first mortgage on the whole property, land and improvements, paying market interest rates and some points. Then the developer sells the property with a simultaneous leaseback. It is this sale that provides the 100 percent financing.

Benefits

The developer gets almost total financing in either case, either before he builds, or after. He also gets the cash flow after expenses and amortization, increases in rents, plus management and maintenance income and the profit from putting the transaction together. In our first example the lender gets a higher rate of return by owning the land because he will get escalation clauses that will increase his rate of return over a fixed interest rate. Also, he will own the land as it increases in value, thus building his portfolio at the same time it gives a market return. The buyer in the second example gets a secure investment with the developer signed on a leaseback and the normal benefits to the ownership of real estate.

Example

A developer owned a parcel of PUD (Planned Unit Development) land in our area that he had purchased five years ago. He still owed $15,000 on it. He had developed his plans for it to have a shopping center and 200 apartments. Other projects had his cash tied up, but he was ready to go to work on this one now.

The lender had money for projects like this but was worried about fluctuation in the interest market and wanted some participation for protection.

The developer sold the land to the lender for fair market value, which made him a nice profit. He then leased the land from the lender for sixty-eight years with a cost-of-living clause in it, and 2 percent of the gross rents. The land was initially to yield 12 percent per year on the price paid for it by the lender. Then the lender loaned 75 percent of the cost of putting up the improvements. With the money from the land sale (and the profit) and the 75 percent loans, the developer had enough money to completely build the center and units with no other capital.

Good Use: Many investors in real estate are simply looking for cash to use in other ventures and decide to sell their real estate to get it. If their strongest motivation is to get the cash, you can often arrange a sale and leaseback so they get the money they require and lease back their property so as to maintain a continuity of management. You can also work an exchange and leaseback with the same advantages. Be very careful if you try to insert an option for either party to buy back their original property—IRS may construe the whole transaction as a loan and not a sale.

26

The Velvet Hammer: How to Turn a Leaseback Into a Triple-A Guaranteed Leased Property

This technique developed out of a common practice where an owner sells a property and agrees to lease it back so as to get the highest price in the marketplace. This provides an investor with built-in management and virtually no problems. After consummating the transaction, however, the seller runs into trouble and defaults on the lease. This leaves the investor with management problems he didn't want and with no way to be compensated for the default, especially if the seller had nothing left, or went under.

The velvet hammer simply means that someone is struck a blow for not performing according to the terms. And it is the person leasing back the property who gets the hammer if he fails. Let's see how it works.

Suppose Able has a forty-unit apartment house that he wants to sell or exchange at top market value. He is offering to lease it back to provide a management-free investment. Your client is a taker for the units and the leaseback. In the transaction you insert the velvet hammer. It provides that if Able does not perform as specified in the contract, your client can step in after proper notice and take over the apartments himself. At the same time, he subtracts some of what he owes Able on their contract balance because of Able's failure to perform as specified. Let's use these figures:

Purchase price of	$500,000
Down payment of	80,000
Able's second trust deed of	70,000
Existing loan balance of	$350,000

At the time of default by Able, Baker still owes him $50,000. The terms of the velvet hammer are that Able is to lose $20,000 if he defaults on the leaseback terms. When Baker gives notice to Able that he has not performed according to the terms of the agreement and it is agreed the terms have not been met, then escrow deducts $20,000 from Able's contract and Baker now owes him only $30,000. This is simplified in its explanation, but that is the essence.

Actually a number of legal steps must be taken before you can deduct the $20,000 unless Able agrees in writing to the default. It can lead to a lawsuit, of course, but is generally avoided by the clear language used in the "velvet hammer" description.

Example

Able had a forty-five unit apartment house for sale at $500,000 with a loan of $350,000. He wanted a lot of cash as he was going to change jobs and wanted some cash behind him when he did so. Baker came into the picture with about $80,000 in excess cash from a farming operation to use to acquire tax shelter. His broker saw the potential in the forty-five units and asked Able to lease them back due to the high rent schedule Able had on them and the fact that Able had set up such a good management team. Able agreed to lease the units back provided that Baker put enough cash down to pay the broker's fees and leave Able $65,000. They agreed.

Baker's broker then inserted the velvet hammer and Able agreed to that. The hammer said that if Able defaulted on the terms of the leaseback, the escrow was authorized to deduct $20,000 from the balance Baker owed to Able. They were able to do this only upon the presentation of a written statement signed by both parties and notarized or upon a court decision. If it had to go to court, the loser was to pay attorney's fees and court costs for the winner.

Obviously Able has a great deal of motivation to perform on the leaseback. He loses $20,000 in paper if he doesn't.

Benefits

Able gets a maximum cash price with the leaseback and a penalty if he doesn't perform. It probably brings the price down to what it would have been without the leaseback by deducting the $20,000. Baker, on the other hand, gets a management-free investment and a deduction if Able defaults. It should work out well for both.

27

Sale and Buyback—and Exchange and Buyback

This technique has a number of applications which, when used properly, provide a great deal of benefits to both parties to a transaction. As the name implies, there must first be a sale or an exchange. Then the person who made the sale or exchange turns around and becomes the purchaser of the property he has just sold or exchanged.

The reasons for doing so are many. By selling, he can establish a gain in an otherwise bad year, thus offsetting his gain tax. He may make a tax deferred exchange with a property, thus getting a new and higher basis in another property, and then buy back his old property and get a new basis on it. The main reason is to raise cash. So, Able sells his property, gets the cash he wants, and buys it back or agrees to buy it back somewhere down the line.

By doing so, he provides the purchaser with some benefits. Let's say the purchaser has money sitting in the bank and he wants to earn interest higher than bank rates. By buying the property offered from Able, he invests his money in property. Now Able buys it back at a little higher price to allow for costs, and a higher return to Baker, and now Baker has paper at a higher rate of return than he was earning in the bank.

All very tidy, except that the IRS has something to say about the buyback. In the first place, there must be a legitimate business reason for the buyback in order to get the new higher basis to depreciate. You see, when Able sold his property he had to pay gain tax on any gain, so the IRS looks more favorably on the deal when Able buys back and establishes a new basis for depreciation. Now, let Able make a tax-deferred exchange under Section 1031 of the Internal Revenue Code, and then buy his old property back, and the IRS does not like it at all. The reason is that the taxpayer has not only avoided tax on any gain in the exchange, but he then buys back his old property and immediately gets a new basis to depreciate. This must be done properly and with the expert help of your attorney and tax accountant, or it will be called a loan by IRS and the new basis will be disallowed. But it can be done properly.

Know How Item

We have several ways of making the sale and buyback work. Starting with the simpler ways, let us assume these circumstances: Able owns a piece of land that he purchased for $20,000. His land has now appreciated to $50,000 and he wants to put a building on it, but he lacks the funds. He approaches the realtor and they decide to effect a sale and buyback. The land is sold to Baker for $50,000 cash, which gives Able the money he is looking for. Now Able buys back the land with a very small down payment, getting subordination rights and the right to substitute other paper for this paper so as to be able to render the land free and clear at some later date. Able gets cash and good terms on the land buyback. Baker gets a profit on the saleback to Able, and he also gets higher interest than he would have made in the bank.

Another method of sale and buyback might be as follows: A professional man owns his own building valued at $100,000 with a small loan of $25,000 against it. He needs to raise at least $50,000 cash for another venture and approaches a realtor to sell his building to raise the cash. The intelligent realtor finds that the professional man really doesn't want to be rid of his building. Selling his building is merely his way of raising the cash he needs. By showing the client the advantages of keeping his building and explaining how a sale and buyback would benefit him, he agrees to pursue that line. The realtor gets a loan commitment of $60,000 on the property and procures a buyer for $90,000 with a $30,000 down payment. With the $30,000 down payment and $35,000 from the loan, less broker's fees and loan costs, the client ends up with about $58,000. And he still has his building, which he buys back at $95,000, giving the seller a $5,000 profit and a higher interest rate than he would have earned from the bank.

Know How Item

In an exchange and buyback we could look at typical circumstances. Able owns a fourplex that is free and clear in which he and his wife live. They are in their mid-40's and are on an estate building program. They like the neighborhood and love the fourplex, but they need to get moving to meet their objectives, so they reluctantly approach the realtor with the idea of exchanging out of it into something bigger. Other ideas are discussed, but the best one seems to be to make a tax-deferred exchange with the fourplex and then let Able buy it back, thus keeping their home and getting a new basis to depreciate, plus boosting their estate building program.

Able exchanges the $100,000 fourplex free and clear on Baker's thirty-six-unit building for $700,000, giving Baker the difference in a second trust deed. There is no statement in the exchange agreement that Able will buy back the fourplex—it is a gentleman's agreement. After closing the first exchange, the realtor opens up another escrow in a different escrow company and makes the buyback work. Stay clear of putting the buyback agreement in the original exchange agreement. It must be an arm's length transaction, which does not require either party to buy or sell after the original exchange is made.

Benefits

Generally the benefits to the seller are that he gets to use the equity in his property to acquire cash. More cash than he could by refinancing. Then, when he has gotten the cash he gets to buy his property back on terms and conditions that allow him most of the benefits of owning that property. The purchaser generally is motivated by a profit in the resale and also in getting higher interest than normal from putting his money in a bank or savings and loan.

Example

Able had owned a warehouse for nine years. It was now valued at $60,000 and leased 100 percent. He owed $14,000 and the property showed a good cash flow. He badly wanted fifty acres of land that adjoined his home place. The warehouse was not highly financeable and his basis had deteriorated over the nine years, a basis that he did not mind transferring to the fifty acres. He exchanged the equity in the warehouse for the fifty acres, giving some cash along with it. Baker, who owned the fifty acres, did not want the warehouse, so Able agreed to buy it back after close of escrow. They agreed, acted, and both were happy. Able got a new basis in the warehouse and now had leverage going for him because he bought back the warehouse with 15 percent down payment. Baker not only got good second paper, but he got an override on the interest rate on the first $14,000 loan. Interest on the first was 10 percent and Baker carried back a wrap-around trust deed at 11 percent, thus earning 1 percent interest on the first loan's money.

28

How to Create Cash by Discount Sale and Lease Option and Still Retain the Benefits of the Property

A seller has had his property on the market for some time but it has not sold due to the poor financing under it. The loans are for a reasonable amount, but the payoff terms are using all of the cash flow and any potential purchaser finds it difficult to accept no cash flow. The seller is asking for a 30 percent down payment and this is killing any and all purchases and exchange offers.

The seller is baffled. He still needs the large amount of cash his property is worth, but it is not coming from the real estate market. This situation is typical and there are various reasons why the property will not command a high down payment. But there are always people in the marketplace who have large amounts of cash available. They simply need to be motivated to invest it. That is the purpose of this technique.

Know How Item

To get the large cash down payment he needs, the seller must tempt the lender or purchaser with unusual benefits.

Let's say Able has a property valued at $150,000 with a loan of $70,000 and an equity of $80,000. Able offers to sell at the discounted price of $120,000, asking for a $50,000 down payment. The first part of the problem is to get the large amount of cash through the discounted sale.

Have the seller agree to lease back the property from the purchasers, thus creating a nonmanagement income property for the buyer. Generally by doing this, the seller creates a cash flow situation for the purchaser, along with the principal reduction, the appreciation, and the depreciation benefits.

Now to protect the seller, you need to get him an option to regain his property close to the bargain-basement price he let it go for.

The option usually contains a reasonable profit for the purchaser, so that if and when Able buys back the property the purchaser makes a profit by the resale. He also makes a very good cash flow on his invested dollars during the leaseback period, plus the other benefits of ownership.

A typical way of setting this up is as follows: Able agrees to lease back his property after a sale if he gets the cash he wants. The property is sold at a discount (say 20 percent), with cash to the existing loans. Able is to lease back for three years, paying all expenses and paying the buyer 1.5 percent a month on his equity. Able is also to have an option to purchase the property back at the end of the three years for the same down payment the buyer paid. Able will also assume the balance of the existing loans.

Benefits

Able gets cash and a chance to redeem his property three years later, getting the benefits of principal reduction on the loans. He also gets control of the property for that period. Baker gets 18 percent cash flow on his invested dollar and a 20 percent discount on the value of the property if Able does not exercise his option. Also, during his ownership, Baker gets the depreciation benefits.

Example

Able: $80,000 house
 −20,000 first trust deed at 8 percent payable $240 monthly
 −20,000 second trust deed at 9 percent payable $250 monthly
 $40,000 equity

Baker pays: $24,000 cash down payment and assumes loans
 $64,000 sales price

Able pays $240 (1 percent of $24,000 a month) plus the $490 on the underlying trust deeds and all expenses of operation. At the end of three years Able has a purchase option as follows:

Down payment $24,000 (same as Baker paid three years earlier)
Assume first trust deed 15,840
Assume second trust deed 16,066
 $55,906 (repurchase price to Able after three years).

Able paid out $8,640 over the thirty-six months of the leaseback, but he also gained $8,094 in principal reduction. The effective interest rate on the transaction for the three-year period was 7/10 of 1 percent.

Benefits

Able	Baker
1) Cash down payment	1) Depreciation
2) Can write-off lease payments	2) Gets 12 percent cash on cash return
3) Gets any cash flow from operation	3) No management
4) Option to buy back (a) appreciation (b) principal reduction	4) Good buy if option is not exercised.

29

The Blanket Mortgage: How to Secure a Favorable Loan by Using More Than One Property

This is a backup method of getting the financing you want on property. Let's assume, for example, that Able has a real estate portfolio and is trying to raise some cash. The normal method is to see what he owns that he can borrow against or sell rapidly. Deciding to get a maximum loan on a property is the best move to make, and he tries the lenders—to no avail. He can't get enough money from any one of the properties. He is aghast. There is a shortage of mortgage money and they just aren't lending as much or as readily as they used to.

Able goes to his friendly realtor for help. The realtor suggests a blanket mortgage whereby Able puts up more than one property for the security of the loan. The properties do not need to be of the same kind, i.e., apartment houses or houses. You can use land and an apartment house, or a ranch, or all three together.

Able can raise some cash through refinancing, and probably get more than he could on any one property and perhaps more than he could have raised individually on each property. The lender gets more security than he would by making the loan on only one property.

Know How Item

This technique can also work with other than conventional lenders. Imagine a situation where Able is exchanging a $10,000 equity in a threeplex for a $30,000 equity in a nineplex, providing the nineplex owner will lend Able $10,000 in cash for remodeling of the nineplex. The owner agrees, providing he can take a note and mortgage on both properties, the nine- and the threeplex, as additional security for the performance, and that Able buy back the threeplex. Here is a sample of mixing of the techniques: Exchange and buyback; blanket mortgage.

Example

Able was trying to raise $16,000 to finish the remodeling of a sixteen-unit apartment house that he had started before he had run out of money. The conventional lender had loaned all the money he was going to loan, so it was up to Able to scrounge up some more financing or lose the building. He approached some private lenders at the high interest rates and high points, but he couldn't interest them in making the loan. They didn't like the uncompleted state of the project and they didn't like the project. They felt it was not good security for their loan.

During the drive home, Able asked them if they would consider making the loan if they had additional security in the form of a free-and-clear five-acre parcel with a trailer house on it in another state. They agreed, and the loan was put into escrow this way. A single note was drawn showing Able owed $16,000 to the lender. Then two mortgages were drawn, one for each property, and recorded in their respective counties and states. The escrow was set up with a $16,000 balance on each mortgage. As a single payment was made, each mortgage was reduced by that amount, so that Able only paid back the original $16,000 plus interest and both mortgages were retired simultaneously.

In a backside operation of this same technique Able owns 160 acres of land free and clear. He wants to buy the 160 next to him but doesn't have much money to do it with. He offers $80,000, which is the asking price, with $10,000 down, but the seller rejects the offer, feeling that is not enough of a down payment and the costs would be too much to foreclose on it. Able then adds his own 160 acres free and clear as additional security for the $70,000 debt, making a blanket mortgage over the ranch he is buying and his own ranch. Seller accepts. Deal closed.

30

The Wrap-Around: How to Secure New Financing Without Disturbing Existing Financing

How would you feel if you had a 5 percent Prudential Life Insurance Company loan on your house in the amount of $15,000 that was put on in 1963 and your house was now valued at $100,000. But you need some money to pay your income taxes and the interest rate on home loans is now 12 percent—a 7 percent increase. You would do about anything you could to keep your interest charges as light as possible, wouldn't you? Right!

The wrap-around mortgage comes into play under such circumstances. Generally, the wrap-around mortgage is used to raise money with an existing old loan bearing an interest rate considerably below the present market interest rate. Into this breach comes some kind of lender: conventional, private, or some corporate structure.

Know How Item

The lender will loan you some money above that amount now on your property. The lender assumes the existing loan and supplies the additional money. The overall interest rate will be somewhat less than the going rate because of the leverage on the existing loan. For example: Let's say Able has a $100,000 house with a $40,000 loan on it at 6 percent interest. He wants a $70,000 loan. The interest would normally be 12 percent. A refinance would get the same amount of money and the lender would now have a first trust deed for $70,000, but poor Able would be paying 12 percent interest. So, by getting the lender to assume the first trust deed at 6 percent, the lender can then lower his rate of interest to Able and still come up with the same return on the money he borrowed. The lender assumes the first loan so that Able is no longer responsible for that. Then the interest rate is computed so that the lender can make the market interest rate on only that money he funded, *plus* a small override on the existing loan of say ½ percent. This figure would be considerably below the current rate.

Example

Able had a sixteen-unit apartment house that he had owned for eleven years. It had an old 8 percent loan on it with an equity of about $200,000 and a loan of about $200,000. He wanted to pull $100,000 out to help build a motel. The lender who had the present loan would have loaned the money, but they were out of funds and didn't know when they would have enough money to make the loan.

Another lender had that type of money available and wanted to have Able for a borrower anyway, so they offered the wrap-around mortgage. They took over the 8 percent loan and funded Able the additional $100,000 at an overall interest rate of 1.25 percent below the current market rate.

Benefits

The borrower gets additional money at less than current interest rates. The lender gets a little more than current interest rates due to the leverage on the underlying loan.

# 31

How to Syndicate the Loan and Get More Than One Lender in the Picture

---

Able owns a property free and clear in a small town, say a motel, hotel, or café. It is not the sort of property that can easily be financed, even in reasonably good times. This parcel also has some additional land that really must be developed in order to make the whole property profitable. Able cannot get a loan from any of the conventional lenders, but he has discovered several brokers who put out small amounts of money for their clients on first mortgage loans. The goal is to get enough financing to build on the additional land so as to make the project rewarding.

Able then approaches the brokers and persuades them to get first mortgage money from their lender clients. By getting enough of them together, he can secure the same amount of money as he would have from one large lender.

Able gets ten lenders with $10,000 each and he syndicates the loan. Each of the investors puts up $10,000. In return for his cash, the investor gets a $10,000 note and a one-tenth interest in a first trust deed. The trust deed is held in escrow and the one payment of $1,000 a month comes in and is distributed by escrow to each one-tenth interest holder at $100 a month each. A default on one is a default on all.

Benefits

The smaller investors can get a piece of a larger, more secure commercial loan and get their money out now instead of waiting for smaller deals to come along. Also, they can put up any amount of money they choose. Instead of $10,000 for a one-tenth interest, they could put up $7,000 for a 7 percent interest, etc. The amount they loan can vary. The borrower gets the flexibility of having many different lenders and oftentimes he can work with individual ones to move their loans to other properties or to borrow more from them at a later date. Often the lenders' circumstances change, such as a move to another area, and they are willing to take a discount to get their cash back or are willing to take other property such as a car or other paper instead.

Example

Able had an acre of commercial land in a town with 3,500 population with a small café and an eight-unit motel. He could not interest any lenders in the project, partly due to the size of the town and partly because they were very short of commercial money to lend and wished to keep what they had for regular borrowers and local people. He went to a number of realtors to see what thoughts they had and along the way asked each of them if they acted as loan brokers for people in their circles.

When he had finished his survey of ideas he retraced his steps and invited the brokers to make his loan available to their lending clients. They could lend any amount they wished over $5,000 and get a note and a percentage interest in the first trust deed on the property as it was to be developed. If he did not get the $100,000 he needed, the money would be returned within ninety days. The brokers were able to secure that amount of money and the loan was syndicated. Each put out only a small portion of the total and shared the risk together.

Caution: Stay clear of advertising in the paper your desire to syndicate a loan. It may be interpreted by the Securities and Exchange Commission as soliciting more than twenty-five people for an offering, since they will probably look at the entire circulation list of the paper as having been solicited for the investment possibility.

Know How Item

This method also works well on large projects where one lender does not want all the risk or does not have the capital needed. It is especially useful on older improved properties that conventional lenders shy away from, such as motels, single-use properties, hotels, and properties that are basically sound but that need renovation. Try and get in your trust deeds the right to substitute other paper at the same payment and interest rate so that paper accumulated over the next three to five years might be used to acquire free-and-clear title to property with the syndicated loan on it.

32

C.D. for Loan—How to Get A Lender to Make a Loan He Wouldn't Ordinarily Make

C.D. stands for certificate of deposit. It is a sum of money put into a bank or savings and loan association for a specified period and draws more than passbook interest rates. It earns higher interest because the bank knows how long it is going to be there and can plan on lending that money out a bit longer, thus earning more on it. The bank can pass some of these additional earnings on to the depositor.

The idea behind using a C.D. for a loan is to motivate the lender to make a loan where he would normally be a little hesitant to do so. For example, Able has a house in a coastal resort area that has a history of landowners who live 100 miles away from their resort houses in the area. Lenders have had problems with loans during the winter season because some houses are rented and some are not, and vandalism and disrepair through neglect and wet weather take their toll. As a result, they are not thrilled at the idea of making a loan to a nonoccupant owner and they resist offering this type of loan.

The property is economically sound and Able wants to raise the loan. He offers to put $5,000 into a C.D. for one year, providing the savings and loan will make him the loan he is seeking. They agree; he puts in the C.D.; they make him the loan; and all live happily ever after.

Caution: You *won't* live happily ever after if you abuse this technique. It is known that people deposit the C.D., get the loan and then pull the C.D. out and leave, letting the poor banker ride on his luck on the loan. Most banks and savings and loans have tightened up this provision now, so that removal of the C.D. is very difficult in less than the designated time limit, unless the depositor can prove a hardship and a strong need to use the money.

Benefits

The borrower, of course, gets the loan he was seeking and even though he has to deposit some money in the lending institution to get it, he still earns 10 percent or better on that money while it is in there, and he gets a loan he would not otherwise have gotten. The lender gets the C.D., which hikes up his deposits and makes his bank grow. It is also an amount of money that he can count on being there for a year, and this allows him to make more money by lending it out than he could on demand deposits.

Example

Able owns an old house that has been converted into four rental units. Behind the house is a twenty-year-old, eight-unit apartment house in a bad state of repair. The present loan is $80,000, but it used to be $160,000 and it is amortizing at $1,600 a month at 10 percent interest. Because of the disrepair the earnings have dropped, and $1,600 a month is more than the property can produce for amortization. It must either be renovated so the rent will produce the money, or the monthly payment must be reduced so it can carry itself. Able chooses the latter course.

C.D. for Loan: How to Get a Lender to Make a Loan

No lenders will loan on that old a property in that condition. Able is seeking an $80,000 loan payable at $800 to $850 a month. He approaches a lender with the thought of putting $20,000 into a C.D. for one year in return for a loan commitment on the terms he is seeking. The C.D. earns 10 percent interest and the bank lends him $80,000 at 11 percent interest, allowing the payment plan he had worked out and giving the property a little spendable.

Know How Item

This works especially well in areas where you are unknown and the lenders are leery of strangers anyway. Putting cash in their institution shows them that you are intelligent and makes them very happy. You can often get them to make the loan by telling them that from the loan proceeds you will make a C.D. in their bank of $15,000 to $30,000. This works especially well on trade-in properties that are free and clear which you are certainly not going to occupy yourself, and for which you have no owner-occupant available.

You request a $60,000 loan on a $80,000 free-and-clear house, and tell the lender you intend to deposit $20,000 in a C.D. with him from the loan proceeds. You pocket the $40,000, put the $20,000 into the C.D., thank him and leave. When you get home you go to your banker and ask to borrow $20,000, using the C.D. up there for security for the loan. The plan works. You are happy—and best of all, you know where the $20,000 is coming from to meet that loan payment when it comes due a year from now.

33

Raise the Interest and Lower the Price

Most of us are so wrapped up in the conventional ways of doing business that to change that thought pattern is a monumental task. But it is well known that the terms on the transaction are every bit as important as the price. Many an investor understands the wisdom of the statement, "You name the price and I'll name the terms." It goes without saying that terms go hand in hand with the price, making it reasonable or unreasonable.

By increasing the interest on an investment the purchaser can pay considerably more for a property in the long run. Taking a property at a set price and playing with the interest rate either increases or decreases the total amount of money that will be paid for it if it is held through its final amortization. This technique is used to give a high-priced seller the same number of dollars for his property, but it gives the buyer a deductible amount of interest instead of a higher basis which is depreciated slower.

Know How Item

When the seller has the price quite high on a property and your buyer refuses to pay that much for it, point out to the seller the savings he will make by reducing the price but charging a higher interest rate. If the buyer is in a high tax bracket, the higher interest rate will be deductible anyway. A married taxpayer in the 50 percent tax bracket only pays 6 percent for a 12 percent interest factor anyway, after taxes. You can figure this out easily by taking the principal amount on an amortization chart and seeing what the payment would be if at the seller's price and his interest rate. Then look up the same payment for the same number of years on a higher interest chart and go back to the reduced principal amount.

Example

Able owned an apartment house that he and his wife were tired of managing. He was retired and wanted to be free to do more fishing and traveling. He was asking $300,000, but the market indicated a value of about $260,000.

Baker wanted an investment in that area but balked at the inflated price. Baker was in the 50 percent tax bracket and had a good cash flow that he could use to pay interest. Baker made an offer at $260,000 using an interest rate of 12.18 percent, which was 2 percent more than Able was asking. The figures looked like this:

$300,000 at 10 percent = $2,895 per month for 20 years;
$260,000 at 12.18 percent = $2,895 per month for 20 years.

Baker also inserted a clause allowing him to pay off the balance at any time he wished. Able could accept the first two provisions but wisely reasoned that if Baker could pay off the loan at any time, he would be left $40,000 short. He could not allow pay-off for a certain reasonable time. Both agreed to no pay-off for the first ten years, and then a decreasing penalty for pay-off during the last ten years.

Benefits

Able got almost the same amount of money from his sale by discounting his price and increasing the interest rate. He would get the same number of dollars if the loan amortized for the full twenty years. Best of all, he had a taker for his units who was financially capable. Able would not have to worry about payment.

Baker got the use of prepaid interest going into title on the property and he also got interest deductions that were tax deductible, which increased his after-tax benefits from ownership of the apartments. It's true he was locked in for ten years, which might present some problems down the line, but a number of conventional loans are that way now and they seem to be working out all right.

34

Lender Loans 75 Percent of Appraisal or Sales Price— or Does He?

Realtors all—what have you heard since you opened your office doors to lenders? "We will loan 75 percent of the sales price or of our appraisal, whichever is less," right? Right! Well, here's something they don't consider: the interest rate. In Chapter 33 I showed you how, by increasing the interest rate, the price could be lowered and the seller would still receive the same number of dollars. Here is the reverse of that situation.

Know How Item

The idea here is to get as much money as possible from a conventional loan. You may need it for remodeling or for staying power while you wait to fill it, or for any of the many reasons for which cash comes in handy in this old world. Let's say that Able owns a free-and-clear property that is really worth more than he is asking by a replacement cost appraisal. But due to his use of it, or the lack of income, or the fact that the property is vacant, it will not command that much in the marketplace.

Baker offers more than the sales price of the property but offers a below-market rate of interest, thus giving Able the same number of dollars if held for the full time. He proposes to take a maximum loan out and give Able some of the cash. The rest of Able's equity will be taken covered by the use of paper.

Benefits

Able gets a taker for his property. He gets some cash and some good paper for his equity. By accepting the sale of his property for more than he asked for it, he also gets an increase in his financial statement, since statements do not require any information on the terms on the paper. Baker raises cash from his paper, gets the use of the property with all of its accompanying benefits, and has the privilege of paying off the balance at the discounted rate.

Example

Able was a widow who was trying to run a small business in a building she and her husband had built eight years before. The business did not need all of the building and she was not doing well with it. She had enough to retire comfortably and there was no reason for her to continue to operate it. The property was appraised and assessed by the county at $109,000 but due to overbuilding, lack of use, and the fact that it had been on the market for a year without any offers she had lowered the price to $75,000.

Baker had a property valued at $120,000 with a $70,000 loan on it that was due, and he could not raise the money to pay it off. None of the lenders in that area would loan on it due to the nature of the property and its mostly unimproved state. He had to raise at least $70,000 cash to pay off that loan.

How to Increase Loans Based on Appraisal Price

Baker, using the created paper formula, offered a created first trust deed for $75,000 for Able's property, free and clear. He made a condition that he be able to borrow $70,000 to pay off the first that was due on his property so he could deliver Able a first trust deed. Thinking with the appraisal by the bank at $109,000 he should be able to get a loan of $75,000 at least, they proceeded.

The bank, of course, came back with the 75 percent of sales price or appraisal, whichever was least. Well, that shot that—or did it?

75 percent of $75,000 = $56,250 . . . not enough to do the job.
75 percent of $95,000 = $71,250 . . . enough to do it!

Baker came alive. His first offer had been $75,000 at 12 percent interest. That made payments of $826 per month. If he offered $95,000 at 9 percent interest, the payments would only be $856 a month for the same period—only $30 more a month. If the bank would accept the $95,000 purchase price, then their appraisal of $109,000 and the sales prices of $95,000 would mean they should take 75 percent of the lower price or $95,000. This would provide a loan large enough to accomplish the need and yield over $70,000 to pay off the old loan.

Baker resubmitted the loan application showing the increased price, and the bank came through with their loan of $71,250. They did not care about the interest rate, only the purchase price and payment terms. I have since talked to several lenders, and they agreed they too would have made the loan.

Baker gave Able $10,000 cash from other sources so she had enough to move with and feel comfortable. Since she was looking for additional cash, they made a payoff bargain. If Baker should want to pay the entire paper off within the first year he could do so for $65,000 ($75,000 minus $10,000 cash given to her = $65,000 at the old asking price).

During the second year Baker could pay the existing balance on the trust deed less $9,000; third year the balance less $8,000, and so on through the first ten years. It was to Baker's benefit to pay off the created paper in the early years if possible.

35

Performance Mortgage: How to Base Your Payments on the Performance of the Property

The performance mortgage came about because of the difficulty in determining income and expenses from some types of properties. This is often the case in Mom and Pop motels, restaurants, grocery stores, taverns, and nightclubs. The owner of such properties may say the income is higher than he reported and the expenses were never that heavy. He may say, for example, that the income from the ice machine or the washer and dryer or the vending machines is not reported and, of course, there is the motel owner who does not report two or three rooms per day. You have only his word on that, however, and if he has lied to the Internal Revenue Service you wonder out loud if he is lying to you, too.

Know How Item

When in doubt about the income and expenses of a property, try and make the mortgage carried back by the seller a performance mortgage, one that will pay based on the performance of the property in relation to the income and expenses that you know to be true. Normally you will base the basic payment on the income and expenses that you have proven to exist, and this payment will be lower than the seller is willing to accept. Then, the mortgage carries a provision in it that lets the seller's statement operate. Any income received above and beyond the proven amounts will be distributed between the buyer and seller in some form. Usually the seller will get the larger amount of the overage. The distribution percentage can stay the same or it can be graduated or reduced as the months go along.

Example

Able owned a motel, restaurant, bar and trailer park combination in a small town. Due to his poor health and general "don't care" attitude, the business had run down considerably. Also, he was not reporting all of the income. He *was* reporting all of the expenses, but his expenses were less than they should have been because he had not taken care of the place and it needed a lot of work—soon.

To offset the need for greater expenses and the income Able claimed was there but not reported, Baker made an offer that included a basic monthly payment of $700. That would cover the first mortgage Able owed to the bank, and it would give Able about $250 per month extra. Then Baker offered to pay Able the balance of his equity as a percentage of the net spendable income above that amount shown on the operating statement by Able.

The percentage which Baker agreed to pay Able was graduated downward. It started with 80 percent of the net spendable income (that figure reached by subtracting the expenses and amortization from the gross income) which was to go to Able the first year. The second year it was to be 70 percent. It declined 10 percent each year until it reached 40 percent. The percentage paid was to level off and remain at 40 percent until Able's equity was paid off in full.

The Wrong Way: The aftermath of this transaction was that Baker put a great deal of money into renovation of the property (about $50,000), which he called expenses. A good deal of the renovation should have been called capital improvements, and only the expenses should have been deducted. So it was that Able did not get any of the extra percentage money for the first three years because of the extensive upgrading done by Baker. They disagreed over this allocation, but it never came to a lawsuit.

The Better Way: Doing it over, we now insert a clause in the contract that spells out what are expenses and what are capital contributions. Baker would then pay the percentage on everything over the expenses. All capital contributions would have to be made out of his percentage left over.

Benefits

Able gets income from payments if he is telling the truth and if Baker can operate the business at least as well as Able did. Baker makes a fixed monthly payment that he feels sure the property can handle, and only increases that amount when the property *has* produced more and Able's claims or Baker's managerial ability have proven themselves.

36

Performance Purchase Price: The Real Way to Get the Seller to Stand Behind the Figures He Gives for His Property

In some situations a purchaser would like to be able to pay for a product based on the salesman's claims—*after* he has bought the product and evaluated its usefulness. Many sellers of properties that have income and expenses find it difficult to part with the really accurate information that a purchaser would like to have. As a result, there is always a degree of suspicion between the two parties to a transaction as to the reliability of the income and expense figures.

This is especially true of taverns, motels, grocery stores, resorts, and other real estate business ventures that allow the operator to hide a certain amount of income. Generally the expenses have been reported to the hilt, unless it is a family operated venture, or they have been doing maintenance and management themselves

Know How Item

Structure the sale or exchange with an undetermined price, allowing for the price to be based on the future performance of the property under new management. Let's say Able wants to buy a motel owned by Baker but can't see paying the price Baker is asking, using the figures Baker has supplied. Baker wants to part with the motel and Able wants to own it, but they are simply hung up on the problem of expenses, income, and price. Not an unusual hangup.

The motel grosses $300,000 a year according to Baker, but Able can only see $250,000 gross in it. To solve this impasse, the broker suggests Able pay a price equal to four times the average of the first two years' gross income (4 x $250,000 – $1,000,000) or (4 x $300,000 – $1,200,000). Therefore, if the motel does gross $300,000 as Baker says it does, he will get paid for it. If it doesn't, Able isn't stuck on figures that he couldn't verify.

Be Aware of These Potential Pitfalls: The problem here could be, of course, that Able isn't the manager that Baker is and therefore the income suffers under his management. Baker needs to be aware of that possibility.

The other problem we have found here is that Able must be reliable and report all income and expenses honestly, something that perhaps Baker did not do. If the price is to be based on net income instead of gross, reasonable accounting methods must be used as well as clear reporting, with definitions outlined prior to going into the transaction about such items as repairs versus capital additions.

Example

Able was a very clever investor who had been injured in an industrial accident and had a lot of time to think things out. He played his cards close to his vest and rarely missed a trick. He wanted out of some apartments and into a tavern which his son-in-law would operate, and he envisioned this last investment of his would give him retirement money without his needing to work for the rest of his life.

The tavern he liked was a little spotty on records and the seller had the typical story about the large number of kegs he sold, his carry-out business, the pool table income, the vending machine income, etc. Some of it we could check and some we couldn't. At any rate, it soon became apparent that to get the tavern Able was going to have to make an offer based on the income that Baker said was there. To protect himself, Able agreed to the following conditions:

1. He would pay 20 percent of the gross income each month towards the contract
2. At the end of two years, the amount that he had paid in would be divided by twenty-four months and the average payment would be the monthly payment.
3. That payment would represent some amount of mortgage that would be amortized over fifteen years at 8 percent interest.
4. Whatever principal amount it represented was the amount that Baker had coming to him.

The first two years Able paid in $58,944 which, when divided by 24, equalled $2,456 for an average monthly payment. That payment used over fifteen years at 12 percent would amortize a loan of $204,638. That's what it did.

37

Such a Business—
You Got It—You Sell It—
and You've Still Got It!

As a takeoff on the old joke, this technique is often used by knowledgeable real estate people to instill capital into a venture or to release some of their equity to acquire cash for other ventures. Meanwhile they maintain control of the property and enjoy a portion of the benefits from it.

Know How Item

The idea here is to let an owner acquire cash for whatever purpose he has in mind, and still retain an ownership and management position. Able owns an income-producing property that has a reasonable cash flow of say 6 percent on the equity. The first step to secure this program is to pull the land out from under the improvements and have Able retain ownership in that. The payments on the land are set up to give Able an asset producing spendable income. It also provides a vehicle for later sale or hypothecation to raise additional cash.

Subtracting the land from the equity will give you the balance needed to cover in this transaction. Let's say the value of the property is $100,000 and the land is pulled out at a figure of $20,000. There is a mortgage on the property of $50,000. The total equity then is $50,000; less the $20,000 for the land, which leaves $30,000 equity remaining.

Generally you would capitalize the improvements at a market figure without the land remaining, but with the land payments included in the expenses. After all, if you are going to have to pay on the land lease it should be considered an expense item.

Now Able sells 80 percent of his remaining equity (80 percent of $30,000 = $24,000) retaining a $6,000 equity position along with the management contract, maintenance contract, and control.

By this maneuver Able has pulled a free-and-clear land parcel out with a cash flow lease on it (value of $20,000) and has sold 80 percent for cash, or $24,000. He can now sell the land lease or borrow on it, raising from $15,000 to $20,000 on that. Altogether he has raised some $40,000, and he still owns 20 percent of the equity in the project, together with the two money making contracts on management and maintenance. If Able owns the entire project, of course, he has access to all of these cash flow items, but not the cash—unless he sells his interest. This was designed to provide tax benefits to an investor and retain other benefits for Able.

Example

Able owned an old hotel downtown that had been converted into low-cost housing for elderly people. The property was valued at $240,000 with a loan of $160,000, which left an $80,000 equity. It was unreasonable for anyone to put up $80,000 in cash to acquire these benefits, so to get the maximum cash out of the project Able did the following:

1. He pulled the land out valued at $30,000 and leased it for a 12 percent return, or $3,600 per year, with increases due to inflation and taxes. The lease was a net lease, so the landowner paid nothing, but his income went up as tax assessments or inflation increased its value.
2. He sold 80 percent of the remaining equity for $40,000 and guaranteed the investor a 6 percent cash flow before he took out anything for his remaining 20 percent equity position.
3. He retained the management of the building which grossed him $14,400 per year.
4. He also kept the maintenance and cleaning contract on the building which grossed him another $3,000 per year.

He had received $40,000 in cash, while retaining the land for sale or holding purposes; picked up $17,400 in supplementary contracts; retained control and got whatever benefits in appreciation, principal reduction and cash flow accrued to his 20 percent equity position. He also enjoyed the sweet depreciation that always flows to the owners of improved property.

Benefits

We have pretty well laid out Able's benefits. The investor gets a knowledgeable real estate man as a partner and he gets first pick of the cash flow, plus depreciation, principal reduction on the loan, and appreciation. He may move with Able to other projects if this works well.

38

Convertible Loan to Equity: A Way to Give the Lender an Incentive to Make the Loan

When arranging loans from insurance companies, union funds, and private lenders, it is entirely possible that you may be able to insert a conversion-to-equity clause, because all of them can legally own property.

Suppose your client is going to develop a shopping center. The feasibility study looks very good and the land is free and clear. Your client needs $800,000 to build.

By giving the lender the right to convert the loan to equity at his option, you provide him with an incentive to make the loan. Since most income-producing properties have a capitalization rate higher than the interest rate on the loan, it could be to the lender's advantage to convert when the property is full and most of the risk is out of it.

Lenders these days are looking for participation to increase their yield, and this is one way to allow them to accomplish it.

Problems come from having a partner who is not knowledgeable in the management of real estate, who owns more of the project than the developer, and who is controlled by a board of directors which doesn't have a personal relationship with the borrower. But the loan is a two-way street and both lender and borrower must get reasonable benefits from the loan.

How to Protect Yourself: Clauses that can be put in to protect the borrower from heavy-handed treatment by a lender are:

1. If lender converts his loan to equity, he becomes a limited partner only.
2. Conversion of loan to equity can only be done with ample notice to borrower.
3. Lenders must join in signing on any new loans—or agree to sell or exchange when borrower wants to sell.

Example

A local builder had a chance to buy some land zoned for apartments at a very low price due to the motivation of the seller and to the fact that the sewer was not yet in.

He checked local lenders and found none willing to loan on the undeveloped land. He then contacted a realtor who guided him to an employees' pension trust fund which provided him with the loan for the land.

The loan agreement contained a clause that allowed the lender to convert the loan to equity and become a limited partner at an appraisal price based on one appraiser being hired by the lender. If the owner didn't like his appraisal, he could then order a second appraisal. If the builder and the lender still could not reach an agreement, the two appraisers were to hire a third appraiser to establish the relationship of percentage of ownership to each party.

Due to a zoning cutback and a master plan drawn up by the community, the land increased in value rapidly, from a purchase price of $16,000 to a value of $24,000 in one year.

The lender made the right moves to convert his loan to equity, and neither party hired an appraiser but instead used the new assessed valuation by the county as fair market value.

As partners, they were still holding the land and were planning to build on it soon.

39

Convertible Loan to Stock: How to Motivate a Lender to Make a Corporate Loan

This is a corporate loan situation. The client you are working with is a corporation and is in need of a loan on some project. The size of the corporation and the liquidity of its stock will determine which lenders you can approach with this proposal.

If you are dealing with a large corporation whose stock is on the market and has a cash market value, then you should be able to talk to any lender. In the event the corporation is a small, local, closely-held corporation and no one has ever heard of it, then your chances with private money are good.

Know How Item

The main benefit in this technique is to motivate the lender to make the loan. Several conditions should be put in the note and mortgage:

1. A specific period before the lender has the right to convert to stock (three to ten years).
2. The treasury of the corporation must have an adequate amount of stock left—and may be required to maintain this stock on hand during the life of the loan.
3. Some provision that prevents the lender from putting all of the stock on the market at once under certain market conditions.

When a local corporation is the borrower, often its stock will rise appreciably and a lender could realize a great deal of appreciation by converting his loan to stock and then selling the stock at the top of the market.

Generally speaking, this technique is used with giant corporations dealing with giant lenders on giant projects *or* the little guys—the three- to ten-person corporations borrowing private money for one project that has a high risk factor. If it doesn't go, the corporation pays back the loan which the individuals have probably had to endorse. If it goes, there is a lot of profit in it and the lender, when he is sure it's going to be a winner, gets off the loan position and takes an agreed upon number of shares of stock for his outstanding loan balance.

The lender's hope is to convert the loan to stock at the time it is rising in value and make more money than he would have at normal interest rates.

It can also benefit the borrower by suddenly giving him a free-and-clear property. The property can be used to provide certain benefits to the corporation such as:

1. Borrow cash on a loan.
2. Sell for cash and paper.
3. Exchange free and clear.

Example

XYZ Corporation was formed to pick up old mining claims. The risk was high, but the potential profit was enormous.

XYZ borrowed from a local corporation. This corporation was formed to borrow money from the bank on a line of credit of $1 million and lend it at about 3 percent more than they paid.

The loan was to buy some gold mining equipment. If the price of gold kept going up and if there was enough gold there and if any of their other various enterprises worked out, XYZ stockholders stood to make big money.

The loan of $60,000 was written to be convertible to stock at the option of the lender. Since all of the principals in the XYZ Corporation knew one another as well as the lender, there was a daily exchange of information.

The loan had annual payments and was converted to stock by the lender just prior to the first payment date. The XYZ Corporation had agreed to merge with a multinational corporation at a considerable increase in the value of the stock.

After the merger, the lender sold the stock and recovered $87,500.

40

Marry an Investor to a User

In the real estate marketplace, generally you can find two classes of people searching for similar investments. The investor is looking for a property that will appreciate, give off some spendable income, give him a tax loss, and provide appreciation by keeping up with the rising inflation. A "user" is a person who needs such a property to provide a place for him to make his business work. The two often have the same building in mind. They seldom have the same plan for acquiring it, for the investor generally has cash, and the user, time and talent—and occasionally some money.

When the property being sold requires a combination of cash down payment and operating capital together with management skills, try this:

Know How Item

No matter who makes the first offer (either investor or user), accept the offer subject to getting the missing ingredient within a reasonable time. I can't recall how many times a client of mine has said he would buy a certain building if I could find a tenant for it. A lot of people would. You simply say to him, "make an offer and I'll find you a tenant."

If the user makes the first offer and the owner refuses to sell because the terms and price are not right, get the offer accepted subject to finding an investor with the cash to make the terms all right. Set up a reasonable time frame for this to happen.

Example

A very energetic, confident young man came into my office one day and impressed upon me that he needed a certain location for his second franchise. He was being pressured by his company to open a second location or face the loss of his franchise in that city. I questioned him closely because I knew the owner of that property would not take kindly to "soft" offers. I soon found out the young man had courage, a good track record, a recent divorce, dressed nicely, had a new car—but no cash.

I wrote up an offer to lease-purchase the subject property. I knew it would be rejected as it was written, but that's the way it had to start. When I presented it to the board of directors, I could tell down in my shoes that it would not fly that way. When they all turned to me and shouted "no," I suggested that they give me ninety days to bring in a buyer who would pay the price and terms they needed.

They accepted the offer that way. In forty-eight days I had a contractor and the beginnings of a limited partnership to buy the building. In the time frame required we had plans for remodeling, adding several new buildings on the land, and a loan commitment for the whole plan.

Weddings are nice. Especially when you can wed the talents of two diverse people together to achieve separate goals.

41

Working Out of Tough Sale or Lease Terms

Able owns a valuable corner property and will either lease or sell it. Your offer to exchange other property for the corner is rejected. Able wants only cash or a strong lease. The lease rate he is requesting is higher than you want to pay and the terms are not to your liking. You must have the corner for your next office building project.

Know How Item

Look for a free-and-clear property on which you can borrow enough money to buy the land outright. Free-and-clear houses work very well for this due to their high mortgage ratios and ready salability. You might even get several.

Offer to exchange the corner land with a lease on it for some houses. Write the terms of the land lease to meet your needs before you offer it to the house owners. Now get a loan commitment on the houses and use that cash to buy out the land.

By closing simultaneously, Able, who owns the corner property, gets all cash (from loans on the houses); the owners of the house get a long-term lease paying a net return on their equity; and you get the corner property with a suitable lease. Now you need to rent or sell the houses with the loans on them.

Example

A corporation owns a corner lot and has a sign on it for sale, lease, or build to suit. A broker responds to the sign and finds out that the owners want $200,000 for the land, will not subordinate to a construction loan, but will take a short-term lease that is not compatible with the use intended for the property. The broker has a client who wants the use of that corner and is willing to pay a reasonable lease rate based on the market. The goal now is to find someone who will accept those lease terms in exchange for something that will generate the $200,000 to buy the land.

A retired General is found with a condominium worth in excess of $200,000 and it is free and clear. The income from the lease on the land would satisfy the General's needs and help him meet his retirement goals better than the cash from the condo.

An exchange is engineered to effect the three-way transaction:

1. The corporation agrees to give up the land for $200,000 cash.
2. The broker's client is willing to execute a lease for a long period, the income from which will satisfy the General.
3. The General gives up the condo for the ownership of the leased land.

Working Out of Tough Sale or Lease Terms 151

The remaining point now is to borrow the $200,000 on the General's condo or sell it and get the necessary cash to close the transaction.

Real estate is like that. You simply have to find the person who needs what the other person has.

42

How to Make Owner Financing Work for You

As no two people look exactly alike, so too, no two financing techniques work exactly the same way. Owner financing is usable in any market. It is especially usable with large equities, lack of financing, a seller who wants higher yields on his money, versatility of terms and conditions of purchase, and in many other circumstances. With that in mind, let's touch on a few ways that the owner-seller can provide creative solutions to financing problems.

Buydowns: A purchaser anxious to get a below-market interest rate can make an offer that includes a large down payment in order to motivate the seller to carry back the financing at a rate of interest that is below the current market rate. This technique is highly usable when sales have ceased due to the high rate of interest charged by real estate lenders.

Example

Our market was slugging along at 14 percent interest with an occasional burst of money at 12 to 13 percent, but nothing a seller could count on. Down payments were the normal 5 to 10 percent of the purchase price. Buyers were having a hard time qualifying for loans because of their tendency to buy at the maximum level for which they qualified to borrow. If a buyer qualifies for a $100,000 loan at 12 percent, he probably won't qualify when the interest rate reaches 14 percent.

Midway into a recent rise in interest rates to 14 percent, a buyer walked through one of our trade-in units and made an offer to purchase. His offer was $85,000 with $30,000 down, and he asked us to carry back the financing of $55,000 at 11 percent. We quickly calculated what current interest was costing us at prime plus 4 percent, countered at 12 percent with a refinance in the next five years, and cemented the deal.

Another Example

A man and his family moved away, leaving a $225,000 house for sale with their agent. When it did not sell, the agent used his commission as a down payment and bought it, thinking he could sell it and make a profit.

He had a lot of interest but no buyers. He also had a $100,000 note due on it in six months. A new company executive moved up from Seattle and, although he didn't fall in love with the house, he liked it enough to buy it. A normal down payment in our area would have been $25,000 to $30,000 for a home at that price. He offered $50,000 down if he could get 10 percent interest. The agent was able to persuade the original sellers to take the $50,000 and forestall the balance of the $100,000 note for two years.

It just goes to show you that money talks in the real estate market. You can always do more with it than without it.

Silent Seconds: In instances where investor financing and owner-occupant financing carry discrepancies in interest rates and terms, a silent second can be used. Normal financing requires 5 to 10 percent down payment and a 90 to 95 percent loan on a home. Often, the seller or builder will accept 20 percent of the price of the home in the form of a note and a second that is not recorded, on which the payments are deferred for up to two years until either the buyer can qualify for a new loan by getting his income up to 3½ times the full house payment, or the home is resold.

Silent seconds are tricky. You don't want to defraud the lending institution or run afoul of state or federal laws. But it never hurts to outthink them and run ahead of them, and that is what the silent second was designed to do. Check with your legal counsel to be current on your state's laws before you do this—and keep abreast of them, as they may change.

Example

Investor financing in our area is about 75 percent of value. Owner occupied financing is 90 percent to 95 percent. Some lenders will not allow a second above their first loan which equals 75 percent of the sales price or the value, whichever is less.

Able wanted to buy a fourplex but because he was an investor the best loan available was 75 percent of value, and no second. The sales price was $160,000 and the loan $120,000. Terms were $15,000 down and the seller was to carry a $25,000 silent second that would not be recorded and on which there would be no payments for eighteen months. This time lapse was to allow the new purchaser to raise the rents so the property could help make the new payments that would accrue on the silent second. If the fourplex was resold in the first five years the second was to be paid in full. Payments started in eighteen months and ran for sixty months or until sold. In the sixtieth month the balance had to be paid or renegotiated to the seller's satisfaction.

Split the Profits: In this twist the purchaser is given title to the home at a price that equals the builder's total costs and overhead, but not his profit. The purchasers pay a normal down payment and buy the home at below market value, but they buy it and get the builder off his construction loan. The builder retains an interest in the house to the extent of 50 percent of the future profits from resale. This allows the builder to recoup his profit later and hopefully get in on some appreciation. The current owners get full benefits of tax write-offs and principal reduction on the loan. This can work on any real estate.

Example

My partner had bid out a house and we built it as a presold. That means we set the price and sold it before we started to build it, something which we had not done before. As we neared the finish of the house, it was obvious we had sold it too cheaply, and if we persisted in this foolishness we would lose about $8,000 on the house. He asked me what we should do. I shrugged. We had contracted and it looked to me as though we were stuck.

He suggested that we sell it to them and put the house in their name but keep a 50 percent ownership in future profits. It would give the buyers all the tax benefits and maybe get back some of our money at a later date. I shrugged again. Why not ask, I thought.

He asked. They mulled it over. They knew they had us if they wanted to persist, but they also knew they were getting a house that would immediately appraise for about $8,000 more than they were paying for it, and they could see our problem. After a weekend they agreed. We hold 50 percent in resale profits allowing us to participate in the appreciation only. Principal reduction and all the tax benefits go to them. We didn't get our cake now, but maybe we'll be able to taste it later.

Land Lease Discounts: When a purchaser buys a home or property, its purchase price generally includes the land and the building. When the land is leased the property can be bought for building value only. Some builders are selling their homes on leased land creating a product that is as much as 20 percent below the price of others. They then pick up monthly land-lease payments that are commensurate with the value of the land. The original price and down payment is less, but monthly payments are about the same.

Example

Let's say the home you want is priced at $160,000 with the land value being $40,000 and the building $120,000. To buy that with a 90 percent loan you will need a $144,000 loan and $16,000 as a down payment. If the builder or seller were to keep the land and lease it to you, the price would be $120,000 and your down payment would be $12,000 with a loan of $108,000.

The land-lease payment would be approximately $267. If you had the loan for $108,000 at 12 percent for thirty years and the land-lease payment, your total payment would be $1,378. If you had the $144,000 loan at 12 percent interest, your monthly payment would be $1,481.

Do more people qualify for a $108,000 loan than for a $144,000 loan? Need I say more?

Balloon Payments: Sellers can often tailor-make the financing to occur with some event in the future. If the purchaser has an aunt or uncle who is going to give him a sizable sum of money at age thirty-five, or he will be selling some asset in a year, the seller can often be persuaded to make an allowance for smaller monthly payments in hopes of getting a large lump sum later on in the agreement.

Example

The seller of an apartment house was asking 30 percent down payment for a very good building. He got a lot of offers but no one offered to pay the 30 percent down payment. He waited. No further offers. Then along came a clever person who offered to make a 7 percent down payment with another 2 percent down the next year; 4 percent the year after that; and 2 percent the year after that. It only totaled 15 percent but it worked. By adding balloon payments along the way, the seller was persuaded to make the sale. He liked the idea of getting some larger chunks of money each year, it fit into his plans. Can it fit into yours?

43

How to Push the Second Mortgage Around to Get the Property You Want

Consider this situation: An owner wishes to exchange his equity in a nice commercial building or apartment house for some land to develop and build some new buildings on. The building he presently owns has a low first mortgage and a small second mortgage. The land he wants to exchange for is owned by a cautious man who does not believe in second mortgages and will not accept the building with a second on it.

Know How Item

The owner can probably remove the second mortgage from his building by approaching the holder of the second and asking him to place it on the land as a first mortgage instead. He may have to pay something to do it, a few points, raise the interest a little, speed up the payoff—but it is a marketable transaction. As the motivation is with the investor and not the second mortgage holder, the terms may change.

Example

A large firm held numerous properties in and around a city. During the last recession several of their office buildings became 100 percent vacant. In order to hold on to them during the two-year lull, they placed small second mortgages on them above the old, low-balance first mortgages. With the resultant cash they paid the expenses and first-mortgage payments.

When the economy started coming back they desperately needed some additional warehouse space and sought land to build one on. They found it. It was owned by a crusty old railroad worker who didn't like debt but needed the cash flow from a rented building. He would not take the building with the short-term, high-interest rate second mortgage on it. The holder of the second mortgage was persuaded to move it from the building to the land and make it a first mortgage instead. For an additional 1 percent of the amount of the loan, they lender moved it and paid for the additional costs of recording, legal work, etc.

Benefits

The building was leased and the railroad worker had a steady income. The holder of the second mortgage made a few bucks by agreeing to move his second to the land and make it a first mortgage. The investors got the land and started preparations for building their new warehouse in the spring.

44

How to Make the Second Mortgage Bring In Cash

Able is selling a property and has a good offer on it, one that he does not want to lose. But the offer is a little short of the cash he needs, and the purchaser is not willing to put up any more cash. In order to make the sale, Able must carry back a large note and second mortgage on the property. Although he is willing to do that, he balks because he isn't getting enough cash to solve his problem.

Know How Item

Instead of taking the entire balance of the equity back in a note and second mortgage (trust deed), have a small note and second mortgage drawn up that can be sold in the discount money market to produce the remaining amount of cash that Able needs. Able then draws a note and third mortgage for his remaining equity balance and keeps that for the resulting cash flow.

If by chance the purchaser should default, Able must be in a position to either continue the second or pick it up with cash in order to protect his third position. But with such a large equity in the third mortgage he would be willing to do so.

Example

An investor who had built a fortune in raw land and was now developing it got into trouble with his bank. They needed $100,000 on some of his notes immediately! He was cruising the real estate market trying to sell one of his subdivisions on pretty good terms.

We were contacted and made an offer supplying $75,000 of the needed cash. He needed another $25,000 net to him. Since he was carrying back a substantial second trust deed, the payments from which he also pledged to the bank, I suggested to him that he create a small second for $35,000, giving all of the payments that were to be made on the second over to make the payments on that $35,000 note until paid, which would take about two years.

He disliked selling paper at a discount, but agreed in this instance. The paper was sold for $25,000 cash and the whole deal closed. The investor's $250,000 plus equity was now a third mortgage, but in three years it would be a second and in the meantime he had the bank off his back and he had room to maneuver again.

45

How to Get Cash By Solving Someone Else's Problems

You have in your portfolio several properties that do not seem to be doing anything for the good of your cause. Your goals are not being met by retaining these properties. Let's say, for example, that you have several free-and-clear lots of dubious value, a duplex that has a negative cash flow, a fourplex that has a negative cash flow, and some personal property such as a boat or car that you have no further use for.

While these articles have value to someone, they no longer represent any useful value to you because they are not being used to their best advantage. No one you know wants them, and even though they have been exposed to the marketplace, there have been no takers.

Know How Item

There are two good ways to put these equities to work for you:

1. Offer some good real estate paper with them that provides enough cash flow to offset the negative cash flow on the duplex and fourplex. Or, create a note and security agreement against some other property you have and give that with the other properties to sweeten the pot a little.
2. Offer to solve someone else's problem. Take on their problem property and offer your various equities in. Give them back a large note and trust deed for more than their remaining equity, *but ask for cash back.*

This second solution offers a variety of openings. Take on a large problem that could excite other investors with a remodel, construction problem, or conversion, and then syndicate the new property.

Example

Able had a duplex, a fourplex, scattered lots, and some small notes. They were owned by a partnership that had been formed to gain equity for five years and then liquidate taking capital gains on the profits.

These small items were not gaining much equity and the two buildings had a negative cash flow. Able proposed to Baker that he take over Baker's condominium project. The condo project was in the depths of depression; Baker had been involved in some lawsuits for a year on the project, had been paying the lender 18 percent interest, and was fit to be tied over the whole thing. He had made no sales in more than a year. There was nothing wrong with the project except the ownership.

Baker had the money to carry the project that far and not much further. He thought Able's offer was a signal from on high. The offer was for Able to exchange his small scattered holdings for Baker's project and give Baker a note that was 30 percent larger than his equity *if* Baker would give the difference back to Able in cash.

The figures looked like this:

```
Able: scattered holdings with equities of ........ $100,000
Baker: condo project with equity of ............ $300,000
      Equity difference owning to Baker ......... $200,000
Able gives to Baker a note and trust deed for  .... $350,000
Baker gives in cash to Able ................... $100,000
```

The reason Baker gives up the $100,000 in cash is twofold. First, he receives a note and trust deed for $150,000 in return for that $100,000 cash. Second, he gets out of his problem—and it will probably cost him more to hang on and do what he has been doing. Not much sense in that.

46

How to Wind Up a Winner by Turning Your Dwindling Stocks Into Real Estate Equities

---

Somebody out there owns stocks that do not have a current value equal to what he paid for them. Some of these stockholders want to get out of the stock market and into real estate. The problem is something like this.

With his first investment capital, an investor purchased some stocks, dreaming that the stocks would rise and one day make him wealthy. But the stocks took the other route. Now, his investment capital has dwindled and the stocks are worth 60 percent of their former purchase value. The investor wants out of his stocks but is reluctant to take a beating by selling them at their present value.

Know How Item

It is an established fact that there are good times and bad times to buy valuable items. If you are a buyer, you are in a better position when the seller is more anxious to sell than you are to buy. If you desperately need a car and buy the first one you see, chances are good that the seller will get his asking price and come out the winner. If you're a money-conscious buyer, however, you will wait until you find a seller who has the car you want and is highly motivated to sell it. Then, you'll buy it for less.

The same holds true for common stock and for real estate. The market for stocks is well known, and prices are quoted in cash daily. The real estate market also quotes prices based on a knowledgeable seller, a knowledgeable buyer, and real estate exposed to the marketplace for a reasonable period. Often, however, sellers do not have a reasonable time, and often a knowledgeable buyer is not available or motivated enough to buy.

Given these circumstances, there are many occasions when real estate can be acquired for less than the appraised price. The object is to find an owner who is highly motivated to sell his property. When he is located, the stock is offered to him as a way out of his property and as a fast-money answer to his needs. The stock can be sold tomorrow and cash can be realized quick. But there may be no cash market for his property. It may take a long time to find a buyer with even a small amount of cash.

Offer the stock to the owner of the real estate at its original purchase price so your investor does not take a loss. The owner will accept the offer if you have determined his motivation accurately. He will then turn the stock into cash and, because he was the one motivated to sell his property, he will take the loss on his real estate, instead of your investor taking it on his stock.

Example

An insurance broker had invested in bank stocks in his early investing days because he could get started with small amounts of

Turning Your Dwindling Stocks Into Real Estate Equities

money and he thought banks stocks would grow. He held a good portfolio of various bank stocks that had gone from $20 or $30 a share, to $40 and $45 a share. When high interest rates forced banks to sacrifice much of their liquidity in 1979, the bank stocks dropped to $10 or $12 a share. He was dismayed at the poor performance of his stocks and he wanted out of them. His ego would not let him take that kind of loss however, and he muttered about it for days.

Finally, I asked him if he would be interested in getting out of the stocks for what he had paid for them by taking real estate equities. He was very much interested.

Next, I found a developer badly in need of cash. He was trying to finish the roads on a subdivision and had borrowed all he could from the banks, had used that up, and needed more. Getting a second loan on the subdivision was almost out of the quesiton. I suggested to him that I knew a fellow who wanted to invest in real estate and could supply some stock which would be readily salable, although I was sure it would not bring on the cash market what the investor wanted for it.

Since the developer had a healthy profit in the developed lots, he agreed to accept the stock at the old purchase price of $20 a share even though he only got $12 for it on sale. With that money he was able to finish the roads and make lots of profit on the other lots. The investor got his original price for the stocks and ended up with good equities in some subdivision lots which he could sell later after they had appreciated.

47

The Ultimate Bail Out

Here is the typical situation in which you can profit from the ultimate bail-out technique. A landowner wants to trade his land, or he is having trouble selling his land. A builder is looking for property on which to construct apartment houses, but he cannot or will not buy the landowner's property. Neither of them is interested in a joint venture.

Know How Item

There are six steps in solving the problem, as follows:

1. The landowner borrows considerable money on the property. Let's say the property is worth $4 million and he borrows $2 million. Assume that his basis is $4,000.
2. The landowner then leases the land to the builder for thirty-five years with the understanding that the

builder will erect a series of apartment houses on the land.

3. As construction is begun on each building, an escrow account is opened. The ultimate lender deposits his funds in the escrow account, the landowner subordinates his land with its thirty-five-year lease to the loan, and the lender buys the existing obligation of the landowner in the name of the builder. Let's assume, for example, that the builder has now borrowed $10 million for construction. The lender from whom he got the $10 million buys the $2 million loan in existence and gives that note, together with the $8 million, to the builder.

4. The builder owns some apartment houses on leased land subject to the financing. He also owns a note secured by a second loan on the land.

5. The real estate involved is then divided into two parts, X and Y, and at that time the X part is released from being collateral for the second trust deed.

6. Then the builder and the landowner make a tax-free exchange, the builder trading his equity in X for the landowner's equity in Y.

Benefits: The landowner realizes several benefits from this arrangement. First, the proceeds from the advance loan remain tax free as the borrowing continues in financing the apartment houses, so there is no mortgage reduction. Second, the changing of the investment from non-income producing land to rental properties is accomplished with no tax to pay.

The builder also benefits. He gets help with the financing of his project by borrowing against the landowner's land, the built-in sale of the X portion of the property, and the Y property to do with as he wishes.

*Example**

The problem could be stated as follows:

Able owns a very valuable piece of land valued at $4 million on which he has a tax basis (cost) of $4,000. He must deal with the problem of the capital gain tax which on such a large gain would amount to 42½ percent of that gain in federal tax and 3½ percent in state tax. To arrange a sale would cost him almost half of his capital. Also, it is very difficult for Able to find a buyer who can come up with sufficient front money to buy the property in a manner that doesn't involve our client Able in the risks of the property's development.

The following series of steps is required to solve the problem

1. Able borrows $2 million on the land from Interim Lending Bank and deposits the money in his savings account at another bank.
2. Then Able leases the land to Baker Building Co. for thirty-five years with a program where Baker will build an eight-section apartment house complex. Able agrees to subordinate his interest in the land to the construction loan that Baker plans to obtain from Take-Out Bank.
3. Baker prepares cost estimates of the project which he submits to the Take-Out Bank, asking for a loan of $19 million. Baker's estimates show a planned total cost of construction of only $16 million, leaving a comfortable margin of profit from him in the loan itself of $3 million. The appraisers for Take-Out Bank verify his cost estimates and the loan officer approves the loan but comes to a pause when the title search reveals a $2 million loan on the land.
4. At that point Able suggests that, since there is a $3 million margin between the cost estimates on building

---

*Considine and Considine, an Accountancy Corporation.

the apartments and the amount of money that Take-Out Bank is willing to loan, the Take-Out Bank buy the $2 million note of which he is the maker from Interim Lending Bank and hold it as additional security for the construction loan. Of course, since Take-Out Bank is buying the note with money that it is lending to Baker, Baker is the real owner of the note.

5. Then Baker completes the construction of the eight-section apartment house complex, files a notice of completion, and Take-Out Bank converts its construction loan into eight permanent loans.

6. Next, Baker divides the apartment houses into two equal groups of four sections. He calls one section the Eastern Group and one section the Western Group. He then releases the land under the Western Group from serving as security for the $2 million loan. Now that the construction period is over, the $2 million loan belongs to Baker. This action is in accordance with the agreement which he has with Able.

7. At this point if we were to inventory the status of things we would find:
   a. Able still owns the land under Western and under Eastern.
   b. The land under both Western and Eastern is leased to Baker on a thirty-five year lease.
   c. Eastern and Western are each subject to a $9.5 million loan made to Baker.
   d. Eastern land is subject to a $2 million loan originally made to Able by Interim Lending Bank but now owned by Baker.

8. At this point the parties make a tax-free exchange:
   a. Able trades his fee interest in the land under Eastern to Baker.
   b. In return Baker gives Able his leasehold interest over Western.

The Ultimate Bail Out

c. Western is now entirely owned by Able subject to the $9.5 million loan and with a basis of $7 million and $4,000.

d. Eastern is entirely owned by Baker with a basis of $16 million (his construction cost) plus $2 million (the loan he made, now secured only by his own property) less the $9.5 million loan he got out of on the exchange, less the $1 million in cash that he took out of the deal, or $7.5 million.

e. Able is out tax free. Baker, as a dealer, cannot make a tax-free exchange and is taxable on the deal.

48

Never Use a Dollar Once

Suppose you find yourself in this kind of circumstance: You have accounts payable of $6,000 and accounts receivable of $2,000. Sound familiar? Let's make it $20,000 to pay and $5,000 coming in to pay it with. Can it be done? It can if you can work the "final spending theory."

Know How Item

Sort bills into two piles. Mark one pile *First*. Into this pile go the bills that are due to places where you borrow. Credit cards, banks, credit unions, finance companies, etc. They represent bills that are on credit and generally revolving or at least they can be reduced and then increased again.

Into the second pile market *Last*, you put the bills that are paid once. Goods and services, utilities, house payments, investment payments, etc. These are bills where there is no extension. No new money comes forth. They represent what I call final spending. Once you send your money to these places it never returns.

The goal in this exercise is to pay the bills where money can be regenerated first. That does two things. It keeps your credit good there and it lowers your account. Once the account balance is lowered you can generally increase it again. Maybe even raise the original limits to some new height.

In the case where you have $20,000 due and $5,000 coming in, you do the following: You pay the bank, the finance company, the savings and loan, and the credit union first with the $5,000. Then you reborrow from some or all of them and pay your CPA, the rent, telephone and utilities. Once there they are never to be seen again.

Example

I once had eight accounts due for a total of $2,000; a finance company was owed $1,000; a bank $2,000; and I had a personal note due of $1,000, for a total of $6,000—all due in ten days. I had $2,000 coming in that I could count on.

I took $1,000 and paid off the finance company; reborrowed the $1,000 from the finance company so that I would have $2,000 to pay off the bank. I then paid the bank and discretely reborrowed $3,000 to meet my obligations on the personal note and the eight accounts that were due.

If I had paid the personal note and eight accounts, I would have been out the money. That would have been final spending. Pay back loans to keep your credit up so you can continue raising your credit limits. You may need to borrow a lot later on. Move your bucks around. Never use a dollar just once.

49

Interest and Points

Interest is tax deductible as an expense. You can write off every dollar of interest paid, dollar for dollar, against income. Do you accept that? Good. Now try this. The American public is taxed by the use of the following:

1. IRS rulings;
2. court decisions;
3. laws.

The Internal Revenue Service makes certain rulings by which they hope to run the taxation business. These rulings are not law, and going counter to them is not an illegal offense. It may invite an audit and you may lose. However, the penalty is not jail, but a fine and interest charges, at worst.

Court decisions are not law either, but they come as close to it as you can come without being statutory law. They are decisions handed down by courts that have jurisdiction in such matters and are intended to define the law in regard to certain individual circumstances. If a taxpayer's circumstances differ from the court decision it is entirely possible that the next court decision may be reversed. Going against court decisions is risky business and may invite an audit, a fine, and extra interest—but not a jail term.

Laws are laws. They are made by lawmakers and are on the books as tax law. If broken they are punishable by jail sentences, fines, interest charges—the whole thing. Do *not* break the laws.

Before you let someone tell you that avoiding income taxes is illegal, you need to understand the difference between the meaning of the words avoid and evade. To avoid is legal. Remember the words of Supreme Court Justice Learned Hand:

> Anyone may arrange his affairs so his taxes may be as low as possible. He is not bound to choose that pattern which best pays the treasury. There is not even a patriotic duty to increase one's taxes. Over and over again our courts have said there is nothing sinister in arranging affairs so as to keep taxes low as possible. Everyone does it, rich and poor alike, and all do right; for nobody owes any public duty to pay more than the law demands. Taxes are an enforceable extraction and not a voluntary contribution.

Evasion of taxes is illegal and punishable and it should be. We need income to run this country of ours, and each of us must contribute something, even if it is only a small amount.

Plenty of people earn only ordinary income and are willing to pay taxes on it. With income producing improved real estate, there are enough other problems inherent in the ownership that the tax code allows certain depreciation benefits to its owners. The code also allows owners to deduct any interest paid on debts on that real estate, just as it allows any other taxpayer to deduct interest paid.

Interest

A taxpayer earns ordinary income. Against that income certain exemptions and deductions are allowed, and he ends up paying tax on a lesser amount than what he earned. The amount that is taxed is known as taxable income. This income is taxed once a year. Most taxpayers, however, send in monthly or quarterly estimates of what their tax liability will be.

Theoretically then, no income is taxed until after December 31 of each year. So income put to use prior to December 31 in a deductible manner reduces the amount of taxable income. Income earned in one year and not used to produce income tax deductions until the following year will be taxed first, because it was the previous year's income, and the deduction didn't come until the following year.

Example

Let's see how this works.

Able earns $30,000 in ordinary income and has $6,000 worth of exemptions and deductions, leaving him a taxable income of $24,000. On December 15 of 1981 he pays $4,000 worth of interest that he owes. His taxable income is now only $20,000. Had he waited until January 15 of 1982 to pay that $4,000 interest, his taxable income would have stayed at $24,000. He would have needed more money to pay the interest in the next year, because he would have paid his taxes on the $24,000, leaving him less than $24,000. If he were in the 30 percent effective tax rate, for example, he would have had only $16,800 left, having lost some $7,200 to the government in taxes.

Let's assume then, for example, that our taxpayer, Able, needs $10,000 in order to operate his household. He can use the balance to invest in real estate:

Gross Income	$30,000
Exemptions and Deductions	−6,000
Taxable Income	$24,000
Less Taxes Paid	−8,000
Income Left to Use	$16,000
Income Needed for Household	−10,000
Left to Invest	$ 6,000

If that $6,000 is invested at a return of 10 percent, the income is $600. Now, if you can invest that income before it is taxed, you would have another $8,000 to work with—more than twice as much—$14,000. If invested at a 10 percent return, the income would be $1,400 a year instead of $600. The investment grows by leaps and bounds, much faster than if you wait for income to be taxed each year and then use only the remainder. The tax laws were written to provide incentive to those who take the risks, and we should make them work that way.

The way to get that income to work before it is taxed is to get tax deductions with it the same year it is earned. That very simply is the concept of using pretaxed dollars. You buy allowable tax deductions with it the same year you earn it.

One more thing: Those tax deductions had better do you some good, because if you just throw them away you lose 100 cents of every dollar. If they hang around until they get taxed you will lose 30 cents of every dollar. So not only should they be invested in tax deductions, but they should be invested wisely and prudently. Any investment where you can get tax shelter is great, but it should also be a decent investment.

The goal then is to use as much of your pretaxed dollars as possible in legitimate deductions for interest. As long as you stay within your personal limits of deductions for investment interest, you have broken no law or ruling. Making offers that are interest only for the rest of the year or offers that have higher interest rates the first year or two to offset a small down payment could be looked upon as reasonable.

The Internal Revenue Code as of January, 1974, stated that a taxpayer could pay the current year's interest and up to one year in advance, providing it did not materially distort the taxpayer's income. It has not been clearly decided what is meant by "materially distorting" a taxpayer's income. What it means is that anything that looks fishy can be looked into under the IRS ruling.

Points: Points are the little added loan fees charged by lenders to the borrower for lending him money. These percentage points are figured on the amount of the loan. A $100,000 loan with 2 points would be 2 percent of $100,000 or $2,000. This is really advance interest for the lender, and the IRS has stated in print that points are to be construed as interest, fully deductible to the party who pays them. They are also added to the interest rate charged and averaged out over the life of the loan to the lender.

Now then, we have two deductible items: interest and points. Let's combine those two deductible items in an investment to see what sort of advantages we might gain by their use.

Example

Able has $10,000 of this year's income to invest. He needs and wants tax shelter—as much as he can get, as quickly as he can get it.

Baker has a $100,000 building for sale. He needs cash—as much and as fast as he can get it. He has a big loss carry-forward from several bad years in a row.

Able	Baker
$10,000 cash	$100,000

1. Able purchases Baker's property on July 1 of the tax year.

2. Able wants to put out as much as he can in interest this year. He offers $2,000 down payment and 20 percent interest only for the rest of the first year plus two points for loan consideration from the seller. He agrees to pay off the loan in four years.

3. Able down payment $ 2,000
   Able pays points   2,000
   Able pays 20 percent interest on
   $98,000 x 6 months   19,600

4. Total deduction for Able in tax year   20,100
   All interest plus 25 percent of the points which are deductible over the life of the loan. Since the loan has a life of four years, you take 25 percent of the points for each of the first four years.

5. Assuming Able is buying an income producing property and that the income from that property will help him make the $19,600 interest payments, along with the $10,000 he had to work with, you can generate for Able some $20,000 in deductions to couple with his depreciation allowance. In the 50 percent tax bracket this could save him $10,000 in taxes.

How to Use Created Paper to Pay Interest and Points

Let's now examine another concept in the use of interest and points—using created paper to pay interest and points. You recall our discussion of created paper earlier in this book where we used the equity in a property as security for paper we offered. A taxpayer can not give a note for the payment of interest. The IRS concludes that the giving of a note has not paid the interest. *But*, a taxpayer can give a third party's note, or a created note and trust deed (or mortgage), for the payment of interest or points, if the other party will accept it.

Example

Look at the interesting things we can do with that. Let's say Able has a farm worth $100,000 with a basis of $20,000 and a loan of $20,000. If he sold his farm he would have to pay taxes on an $80,000 gain. That gain would be taxed, and whatever was left would be put to work for Able.

But now, let's create a note and second mortgage against the farm. Let's make it for $20,000 above the first loan on the farm of $20,000, for a total indebtedness of $40,000, or $20,000 over Able's basis. That second $20,000 is in the gain area, isn't it? If Able uses that created note and second mortgage to pay interest on another investment, he is using untaxed potential gain to acquire this year's tax deductions. Did you get that? How sweet it is—how sweet it is! Where else but in America could you take an untaxed capital gain and use it to get tax deductions?

So it comes down to this. You can use these items to pay interest with: cash, another person's note, a secured note, any mortgage paper such as a contract, mortgage, or trust deed; personal property, stock, bonds . . . really almost anything the other party will accept as interest and be willing to pay his taxes on, except for a personal note unsecured. Makes it pretty broad, doesn't it?

Example

A particular builder did get into some powerful problems after having his contracting business put into limbo by his bonding company. In an effort to get some cash kicked loose he was willing to be most creative. He had several apartment houses he had built and kept and they looked to him like a way to spring loose some equity dollars.

An insurance broker had just made a mint in the first half of that year and was looking for a way not to pay taxes on all of it. The situation seemed made in heaven.

The broker could not get enough tax shelter by just purchasing the apartments to shelter his income. The total purchase price of the buildings and the total debt were also more than he wanted. By some creative thinking on the part of his CPA and the broker involved, the following emerged.

The investor offered to purchase all of the apartment house units from the builder with a very small down payment. Since interest rates were high he offered to compensate for his small down payment by paying a high rate of interest on the overall debt for the rest of the year. Since he did not have enough money to do that in cash, he created a note and second deed of trust against his condominium in Hawaii for part of the interest.

The result was that the builder got some cash in the form of a note and second deed of trust which he promptly sold for a discount. He also got a small bundle of cash for the interest payments because the insurance broker agreed to pay the interest in advance, since he already had it.

The insurance broker got some good apartments for investment purposes, got to deduct a sizable amount of interest on the new purchase, and used some of his dead equity in the condominium to further defray his tax burden.

50

Tax Strategies in Creative Financing

The days are gone when you could make a lot of money and keep it all. Today the worker is taxed two ways. One is on his ordinary income, the money he makes by his labors. The other is on his capital gain, that which his savings may earn for him. Short-term capital gain is taxed at the same rate as ordinary income. Long-term gain is, at the moment, taxed at a somewhat lower rate.

It makes little sense to make a lot of money if you are going to give away a disproportionate share to taxes. The government is entitled to something, but not everything. Therefore, those of us who are laboring to build an estate and acquire personal wealth should pay the least amount of tax necessary.

Know How Item

It is enough to say that money reinvested without being taxed first should produce more wealth than having it taxed at each move.

Before you make a move to buy, exchange, or sell, examine your tax position before and after the transaction. Consult a good Certified Public Accountant (CPA) who can analyze your situation and advise you on your projected moves. Even before you need a CPA, however, you can be on the lookout for tax traps and ways to increase your net worth without having it taxed.

Basis: When you buy some investment property or a home, you will have established a basis. That basis is your original cost. It changes through the years in two ways. The basis goes up according to any capital improvements you add to the property. The basis goes down according to any depreciation you have taken on it in your tax returns.

Set a Small Allocation to Land and a High One on Depreciable Items

Basis is further divided by an allocation of that basis to land, personal property, and improvements (buildings). In most cases the taxpayer comes out ahead here by allocating a low amount to the land which is nondepreciable. This leaves more of the basis for personal property and buildings, which are depreciable, thus increasing the deductions for tax purposes.

Use Component Depreciation: When setting up your tax schedules on an investment property, try to use component depreciation, which allows the property to be depreciated according to its components—that is, roof, parking lot, electrical, plumbing, appliances, carpet, drapes, windows and doors, heating equipment and building shell. It is a fact that these items depreciate at varying rates and can be treated that way if properly done. In order to make component depreciation work, you will most likely need either a new building where these items can be pulled from the cost of construction, or you should have a qualified appraiser, engineer, and contractor go over the building and itemize the component parts according to their present value. (See the Harsh case—Harsh Investment Corp. v. U.S.

1/9/70 DC One for a more definitive treatise on component depreciation of used buildings.)

Setting Up Tax Schedules

Set these components up on short straight-line depreciation. The experts tell me that the IRS computers are programmed to kick out for tax review any item for which accelerated depreciation is claimed. By using the component method of depreciation and using straight-line depreciation, you avoid recapture rules and can still produce a sizable taxable loss without running into unfavorable tax consequences at a later date.

Remember, the issue here is tax avoidance—not tax evasion. There is a big difference. One causes penalties and possible prison; the other is just the normal taxpayer's right. The reason for avoiding taxes is to maximize your capital as it marches toward your wealth goal. If it is stunted by taxes each time you make a profit, it will take you longer to get there and deprive the free marketplace of your capital. It will go to the government, which is wasteful and will not return much to your local marketplace.

Maximize Your Leverage

When you are buying with the help of creative financing techniques, keep your down payment as low as possible to realize maximum leverage. Leverage is described as using other peoples' money and controlling as much wealth as you can with as few of your own dollars as necessary.

Leverage has its disadvantages. It is not all roses. When a downturn occurs in the economy and there is no market for your leveraged land you could have payments due that you can't meet. You could have an apartment house with 60 percent occupancy and payments that you can't meet. You could have a single-purpose commercial building that is vacant due to the unhealthy business climate at the time. Having a few dollars invested in these properties and being leveraged to the hilt will cause you many problems, from sleepless nights to bankruptcy, and many stops in between. I have seen many people bite many bullets with leverage and am no stranger to it myself.

Tax Benefits of Leverage

But leverage does produce tremendous tax benefits. The benefits that accrue to a landlord are as follows:

> **Cash Flow:** that cash that comes from the property after all has been received; all expenses of operation paid; and the debt serviced.
>
> **Principal Reduction:** the amount by which the debt is reduced each year as each payment covers the interest due and then pays something on the principal.
>
> **Taxable Loss:** the loss, for tax purposes, that accrues to the owner when the interest paid on the debt added to the depreciation taken, equals more than the net operating income from the property (net operating income being that income left after all expenses are paid and before debt service).
>
> **Appreciation:** the amount the property appreciates in the marketplace due to
> 1. fewer properties of that sort in the market, and
> 2. general inflation, which raises replacement costs.

Certain benefits are more valuable and useful at different times in our economic lives. When you are middle aged and earning at your highest ordinary income rate, who needs more cash flow? What you need is more tax shelter to cover the ordinary income you're earning. You need appreciation in early years and in middle years—

in fact you always need it to keep your wealth growing with inflation. You get reduction of principal anyway, unless you have an interest-only contract.

Your goals then should be to:

1. Buy with leverage, providing you have arranged for a small backup in case of an economic downturn.
2. Place a low value on the land and a high one on depreciable ones.
3. Use component depreciation instead of composite depreciation if at all possible.
4. Get your cash flow tax free by producing a taxable loss through use of interest payments and depreciation.
5. Get your principal reduction and appreciation taxed ultimately as capital gain (long term) and not as ordinary income.

Exchanging and How It Helps Your Tax Picture

By exchanging properties you can avoid being taxed on your gain—that is, the difference between your adjusted cost basis and the fair market value of your property. If your investment property is no longer giving you the benefits you desire, you can exchange up—up in price and up in debt—and probably pay no tax on the transaction. With inflation and principal reduction and tax-free cash flow, you can manipulate your holdings into millionaire status, tax free. Many investors have done it, and you can, too. It simply takes knowledge, work and persistence.

Exchanging is the subject of many books. My goal here is simply to acquaint you with a few of its fascinating attributes.

Each time you exchange, you set up new allocations for land, personal property, and improvements. You set up new depreciation schedules and start again.

If you sell one property and buy another, you pay on your capital gains. Not so with a properly structured exchange. You can take your capital gain with you to the next property without being taxed on it. It is called "tax deferred." Generally speaking, if you go "up" in price and "up" in debt, you will be free of paying tax in that transaction. You can goof it up (which is why you should seek the assistance of a good tax counselor and a knowledgeable exchange broker), but that is the general guideline.

Example

If you have a property worth $500,000 and if you were to sell it and pay a tax of $50,000 on the gain, that $50,000 would be lost to you forever. But if you exchange and defer the tax, that $50,000 is now continuing to work for you. If the property you receive in exchange is yielding an overall rate of return on equity of 40 percent, that money you would have paid in taxes is now earning you $20,000 a year. Enough said.

Here are just a few ways in which exchanging can help you solve problems.

Vacant Lots Can Solve Problems: You have ten lots that were subdivided years ago and nobody wants to buy them. You can exchange them. It's not difficult to exchange them for "problem" properties where you must step in and solve a real estate problem. Anybody with a problem property will generally take free-and-clear land to get out of his problem.

Cure a Loan Coming Due: Perhaps you own some property that has a loan coming due on it, but you can't get a new loan because the lenders won't loan on that particular type of property now. You stand to lose it if you don't get new financing. You can exchange that property for some other property in some other place that can be financed and pay the loan.

Make a Geographical Exchange: Let's say you have a house in

Nebraska but you have moved to Oregon. You can exchange that house in Nebraska for a place in Oregon.

You can exchange any real estate for any other real estate. The one thing you can't do is pick what you want. But you can pick what you want and wind up with it if you keep exchanging in order to get there.

I often tell my exchange clients that they can't have anything that is on the market for sale unless they have the money to get it with. If they are going to use their equities to acquire property in another area, they must be willing to accept the properties offered by someone who will accept what they have. But they can go on exchanging—and on and on. I have seen as many as fifteen different owners and properties involved in one exchange, where each person put in what he had and ended up with another property which was more to his liking.

Keeping in mind the steps you need to take to improve your tax situation, make your moves cautiously, plan well, and seek advance help and counsel from a good tax advisor and a knowledgeable exchange broker. You can exchange up or down into different holdings. You can move geographically. You can solve financing problems. It simply takes time, knowledge, and a little money for costs.

Selected Real Estate Tables

Simple Interest Table

Example of how to use this table:
Find amount of $500 in 8 years at 6% simple interest.
From table at 8 years and 6% for $1   1.48
Value in 8 years for $500 (500 x 1.48) $740

Interest Rate

Number of Years	3%	3½%	4%	4½%	5%	6%	7%	8%
1	1.03	1.035	1.04	1.045	1.05	1.06	1.07	1.08
2	1.06	1.070	1.08	1.090	1.10	1.12	1.14	1.16
3	1.09	1.105	1.12	1.135	1.15	1.18	1.21	1.24
4	1.12	1.140	1.16	1.180	1.20	1.24	1.28	1.32
5	1.15	1.175	1.20	1.225	1.25	1.30	1.35	1.40
6	1.18	1.210	1.24	1.270	1.30	1.36	1.42	1.48
7	1.21	1.245	1.28	1.315	1.35	1.42	1.49	1.56
8	1.24	1.280	1.32	1.360	1.40	1.48	1.56	1.64
9	1.27	1.315	1.36	1.405	1.45	1.54	1.63	1.72
10	1.30	1.350	1.40	1.450	1.50	1.60	1.70	1.80
11	1.33	1.385	1.44	1.495	1.55	1.66	1.77	1.88
12	1.36	1.420	1.48	1.540	1.60	1.72	1.84	1.96
13	1.39	1.455	1.52	1.585	1.65	1.78	1.91	2.04
14	1.42	1.490	1.56	1.630	1.70	1.84	1.98	2.12
15	1.45	1.525	1.60	1.675	1.75	1.90	2.05	2.20
16	1.48	1.560	1.64	1.720	1.80	1.96	2.12	2.28
17	1.51	1.595	1.68	1.765	1.85	2.02	2.19	2.36
18	1.54	1.630	1.72	1.810	1.90	2.08	2.26	2.44
19	1.57	1.665	1.76	1.855	1.95	2.14	2.33	2.52
20	1.60	1.700	1.80	1.900	2.00	2.20	2.40	2.60
21	1.63	1.735	1.84	1.945	2.05	2.26	2.47	2.68
22	1.66	1.770	1.88	1.990	2.10	2.32	2.54	2.76
23	1.69	1.805	1.92	2.035	2.15	2.38	2.61	2.84
24	1.72	1.840	1.96	2.080	2.20	2.44	2.68	2.92
25	1.75	1.875	2.00	2.125	2.25	2.50	2.75	3.00
26	1.78	1.910	2.04	2.170	2.30	2.56	2.82	3.08
27	1.81	1.945	2.08	2.215	2.35	2.62	2.89	3.16
28	1.84	1.980	2.12	2.260	2.40	2.68	2.96	3.24
29	1.87	2.015	2.16	2.305	2.45	2.74	3.03	3.32
30	1.90	2.050	2.20	2.350	2.50	2.80	3.10	3.40
31	1.93	2.085	2.24	2.395	2.55	2.86	3.17	3.48
32	1.96	2.120	2.28	2.440	2.60	2.92	3.24	3.56
33	1.99	2.155	2.32	2.485	2.65	2.98	3.31	3.64
34	2.02	2.190	2.36	2.530	2.70	3.04	3.38	3.72
35	2.05	2.225	2.40	2.575	2.75	3.10	3.45	3.80
36	2.08	2.260	2.44	2.620	2.80	3.16	3.52	3.88
37	2.11	2.295	2.48	2.665	2.85	3.22	3.59	3.96
38	2.14	2.330	2.52	2.710	2.90	3.28	3.66	4.04
39	2.17	2.365	2.56	2.755	2.95	3.34	3.73	4.12
40	2.21	2.400	2.60	2.800	3.00	3.40	3.80	4.20

Simple Interest Table *(Continued)*

Interest Rate

Number of Years	9%	10%	11%	12%	13%	14%	15%	20%
1	1.09	1.10	1.11	1.12	1.13	1.14	1.15	1.20
2	1.18	1.20	1.22	1.24	1.26	1.28	1.30	1.40
3	1.27	1.30	1.33	1.36	1.39	1.42	1.45	1.60
4	1.36	1.40	1.44	1.48	1.52	1.56	1.60	1.80
5	1.45	1.50	1.55	1.60	1.65	1.70	1.75	2.00
6	1.54	1.60	1.66	1.72	1.78	1.84	1.90	2.20
7	1.63	1.70	1.77	1.84	1.91	1.98	2.05	2.40
8	1.72	1.80	1.88	1.96	2.04	2.12	2.20	2.60
9	1.81	1.90	1.99	2.08	2.17	2.26	2.35	2.80
10	1.90	2.00	2.10	2.20	2.30	2.40	2.50	3.00
11	1.99	2.10	2.21	2.32	2.43	2.54	2.65	3.20
12	2.08	2.20	2.32	2.44	2.56	2.68	2.80	3.40
13	2.17	2.30	2.43	2.56	2.69	2.82	2.95	3.60
14	2.26	2.40	2.54	2.68	2.82	2.96	3.10	3.80
15	2.35	2.50	2.65	2.80	2.95	3.10	3.25	4.00
16	2.44	2.60	2.76	2.92	3.08	3.24	3.40	4.20
17	2.53	2.70	2.87	3.04	3.21	3.38	3.55	4.40
18	2.62	2.80	2.98	3.16	3.34	3.52	3.70	4.60
19	2.71	2.90	3.09	3.28	3.47	3.66	3.85	4.80
20	2.80	3.00	3.20	3.40	3.60	3.80	4.00	5.00
21	2.89	3.10	3.31	3.52	3.73	3.94	4.15	5.20
22	2.98	3.20	3.42	3.64	3.86	4.08	4.30	5.40
23	3.07	3.30	3.53	3.76	3.99	4.22	4.45	5.60
24	3.16	3.40	3.64	3.88	4.12	4.36	4.60	5.80
25	3.25	3.50	3.75	4.00	4.25	4.50	4.75	6.00
26	3.34	3.60	3.86	4.12	4.38	4.64	4.90	6.20
27	3.43	3.70	3.97	4.24	4.51	4.78	5.05	6.40
28	3.52	3.80	4.08	4.36	4.64	4.92	5.20	6.60
29	3.61	3.90	4.19	4.48	4.77	5.06	5.35	6.80
30	3.70	4.00	4.30	4.60	4.90	5.20	5.50	7.00
31	3.79	4.10	4.41	4.72	5.03	5.34	5.65	7.20
32	3.88	4.20	4.52	4.84	5.16	5.48	5.80	7.40
33	3.97	4.30	4.63	4.96	5.29	5.62	5.95	7.60
34	4.06	4.40	4.74	5.08	5.42	5.76	6.10	7.80
35	4.15	4.50	4.85	5.20	5.55	5.90	6.25	8.00
36	4.24	4.60	4.96	5.32	5.68	6.04	6.40	8.20
37	4.33	4.70	5.07	5.44	5.81	6.18	6.55	8.40
38	4.42	4.80	5.18	5.56	5.94	6.32	6.70	8.60
39	4.51	4.90	5.29	5.68	6.07	6.46	6.85	8.80
40	4.60	5.00	5.40	5.80	6.20	6.60	7.00	9.00

Compound Interest Table

Example of how to use this table:
Find how much $1,000 now in a bank will grow to in 14 years at 4% interest.
From table 14 years at 4%   1.7317
Value in 14 years of $1,000 $1,731.70

Interest Rate

Number of Years	3%	3½%	4%	4½%	5%	6%	7%	8%
1	1.0300	1.0350	1.0400	1.0450	1.0500	1.0600	1.0700	1.0800
2	1.0609	1.0712	1.0816	1.0920	1.1025	1.1236	1.1449	1.1664
3	1.0927	1.1087	1.1249	1.1412	1.1576	1.1910	1.2250	1.2597
4	1.1255	1.1475	1.1699	1.1925	1.2155	1.2624	1.3107	1.3604
5	1.1593	1.1877	1.2167	1.2462	1.2763	1.3332	1.4025	1.4693
6	1.1941	1.2293	1.2653	1.3023	1.3401	1.4185	1.5007	1.5868
7	1.2299	1.2723	1.3159	1.3609	1.4071	1.5030	1.6057	1.7138
8	1.2668	1.3168	1.3686	1.4221	1.4775	1.5938	1.7181	1.8509
9	1.3048	1.3629	1.4233	1.4861	1.5513	1.6894	1.8384	1.9990
10	1.3439	1.4106	1.4802	1.5530	1.6289	1.7908	1.9671	2.1589
11	1.3842	1.4600	1.5395	1.6229	1.7103	1.8982	2.1048	2.3316
12	1.4258	1.5111	1.6010	1.6959	1.7959	2.0121	2.2521	2.5181
13	1.4685	1.5640	1.6651	1.7722	1.8856	2.1329	2.4098	2.7196
14	1.5126	1.6187	1.7317	1.8519	1.9799	2.2609	2.5785	2.9371
15	1.5580	1.6753	1.8009	1.9353	2.0789	2.3965	2.7590	3.1721
16	1.6047	1.7340	1.8730	2.0224	2.1829	2.5403	2.9521	3.4259
17	1.6528	1.7947	1.9479	2.1134	2.2920	2.6927	3.1588	3.7000
18	1.7024	1.8575	2.0258	2.2085	2.4066	2.8543	3.3799	3.9960
19	1.7535	1.9225	2.1068	2.3079	2.5270	3.0255	3.6165	4.3157
20	1.8061	1.9898	2.1911	2.4117	2.6533	3.2075	3.8696	4.6609
21	1.8603	2.0594	2.2788	2.5202	2.7860	3.3995	4.1405	5.0338
22	1.9161	2.1315	2.3699	2.6337	2.9253	3.6035	4.4304	5.4365
23	1.9736	2.2061	2.4647	2.7522	3.0715	3.8197	4.7405	5.8714
24	2.0328	2.2833	2.5633	2.8760	3.2251	4.0489	5.0723	6.3411
25	2.0938	2.3632	2.6658	3.0054	3.3864	4.2918	5.4274	6.8484
26	2.1566	2.4460	2.7725	3.1407	3.5557	4.5493	5.8073	7.3963
27	2.2213	2.5316	2.8834	3.2820	3.7335	4.8223	6.2138	7.9880
28	2.2879	2.6202	2.9987	3.4297	3.9201	5.1116	6.6488	8.6271
29	2.3566	2.7119	3.1187	3.5840	4.1161	5.4183	7.1142	9.3172
30	2.4273	2.8068	3.2434	3.7453	4.3219	5.7434	7.6122	10.5582
31	2.5001	2.9050	3.3731	3.9139	4.5380	6.0881	8.1451	10.8676
32	2.5751	3.0067	3.5081	4.0900	4.7649	6.4533	8.7152	11.7370
33	2.6523	3.1119	3.6484	4.2740	5.0032	6.8408	9.3253	12.6760
34	2.7319	3.2209	3.7943	4.4664	5.2533	7.2510	9.9781	13.6901
35	2.8139	3.3336	3.9461	4.6673	5.5160	7.6860	10.6765	14.7853
36	2.8983	3.4503	4.1039	4.8774	5.7918	8.1479	11.4239	15.9681
37	2.9852	3.5710	4.2681	5.0969	6.0814	8.6360	12.2236	17.2456
38	3.0748	3.6960	4.4388	5.3262	6.3855	9.1542	13.0792	18.6252
39	3.1670	3.8254	4.6164	5.5659	6.7048	9.7035	13.9948	20.1152
40	3.2620	3.9593	4.8010	5.8164	7.0400	10.2857	14.9744	21.7245

Compound Interest Table *(Continued)*

Interest Rate

Number of Years	9%	10%	11%	12%	13%	14%	15%	20%
1	1.0900	1.1000	1.1100	1.1200	1.1300	1.1400	1.1500	1.2000
2	1.1881	1.2100	1.2321	1.2544	1.2769	1.2996	1.3225	1.4400
3	1.2950	1.3310	1.3576	1.4049	1.4428	1.4815	1.5208	1.7280
4	1.4115	1.4647	1.5180	1.5735	1.6304	1.6389	1.7490	2.0736
5	1.5386	1.6105	1.6350	1.7623	1.8424	1.9254	2.0113	2.4883
6	1.6771	1.7715	1.8704	1.9738	2.0819	2.1949	2.3130	2.9859
7	1.8230	1.9487	2.0761	2.2106	2.3526	2.5022	2.6600	3.5831
8	1.9925	2.1435	2.3045	2.4759	2.6584	2.8525	3.0590	4.2998
9	2.1718	2.3579	2.5580	2.7730	3.0040	3.2519	3.5178	5.1597
10	2.3673	2.5937	2.8394	3.1058	3.3945	3.7072	4.0455	6.1917
11	2.5804	2.8531	3.1517	3.4785	3.8358	4.2262	4.6523	7.4300
12	2.8126	3.1384	3.4984	3.8959	4.3345	4.8179	5.3502	8.9161
13	3.0658	3.4522	3.8832	4.3634	4.8980	5.4924	6.1527	10.6993
14	3.3417	3.7974	4.3104	4.8871	5.5347	6.2613	7.0757	12.8391
15	3.6424	4.1772	4.7845	5.4735	6.2542	7.1379	8.1370	15.4070
16	3.9703	4.5949	5.3108	6.1303	7.0673	8.1372	9.3576	18.4884
17	4.3276	5.0544	5.8950	6.8660	7.9860	9.2764	10.7612	22.1861
18	4.7171	5.5599	6.5435	7.6899	9.0242	10.5751	12.3754	26.6233
19	5.1416	6.1159	7.2633	8.6127	10.1974	12.0556	14.2317	31.9479
20	5.6044	6.7274	8.0623	9.6462	11.5230	13.7434	16.3665	38.3375
21	6.1088	7.4002	8.9491	10.8038	13.0210	15.6675	18.8215	46.0051
22	6.6586	8.1402	9.9335	12.1003	14.7138	17.8610	21.6447	55.2061
23	7.2578	8.9543	11.0262	13.5523	16.6266	20.3615	24.8914	66.2473
24	7.9110	9.8497	12.2391	15.1786	18.7880	23.2122	28.6251	79.4968
25	8.6230	10.8347	13.5854	17.0000	21.2305	26.4619	32.9189	95.3962
26	9.3991	11.9181	15.0793	19.0400	23.9905	30.1665	37.8567	114.4754
27	10.2450	13.1099	16.7386	21.3248	27.1092	34.3899	43.5353	137.3705
28	11.1671	14.4209	18.5799	23.8838	30.6334	39.2044	50.0656	164.8446
29	12.1721	15.8630	20.6236	26.7499	34.6158	44.6931	57.5754	197.8135
30	13.2676	17.4494	22.8922	29.9599	39.1158	50.9501	66.2117	237.3763
31	14.4617	19.1943	25.4104	33.5551	44.2009	58.0831	76.1435	284.8515
32	15.7633	21.1137	28.2055	37.5817	49.9470	66.2148	87.5650	341.8218
33	17.1820	23.2251	31.3082	42.0915	56.4402	75.4849	100.6998	410.1862
34	18.7284	25.5476	34.7521	47.1425	63.7774	86.0527	115.8048	492.2235
35	20.4139	28.1024	38.5748	52.7996	72.0685	98.1001	133.1755	590.6682
36	22.2512	30.9128	42.8180	59.1355	81.4374	111.8342	153.1518	708.8018
37	24.2538	34.0039	47.5280	66.2318	92.0242	127.4909	176.1246	850.5622
38	26.4366	37.4048	52.7561	74.1796	103.9874	145.3397	202.5433	1020.6746
39	28.8159	41.1447	58.5593	83.0812	117.5057	165.6872	232.9248	1224.8096
40	31.4094	45.2592	65.0008	93.0509	132.7815	188.8835	267.8635	1469.7715

Self-Liquidating Mortgage Payments—Constant Monthly Payment Schedule

The following table shows the constant monthly payment required to liquidate a mortgage loan of $1,000 running for any number of whole years between 5 and 40 years inclusive and at interest rates running from 4% through 12% at 1/4% intervals. All fractions are rounded to the next higher cent, thus making the final payment slightly smaller than the others. This table is especially useful in connection with home mortgages, which usually call for monthly payments.

Years of Loan	9-1/2%	9-3/4%	10%	10-1/4%	10-1/2%	10-3/4%	11%	11-1/4%	11-1/2%	11-3/4%	12%
1	87.68	87.80	87.92	88.03	88.15	88.27	88.38	88.50	88.62	88.73	88.85
2	45.91	46.03	46.14	46.26	46.38	46.49	46.61	46.72	46.84	46.96	47.07
3	32.03	32.15	32.27	32.38	32.50	32.62	32.74	32.86	32.98	33.10	33.21
4	25.12	25.24	25.36	25.48	25.60	25.72	25.85	25.97	26.09	26.21	26.33
5	21.00	21.12	21.25	21.37	21.49	21.62	21.74	21.87	21.99	22.12	22.24
6	18.27	18.40	18.53	18.65	18.78	18.91	19.03	19.16	19.29	19.42	19.55
7	16.34	16.47	16.60	16.73	16.86	16.99	17.12	17.25	17.39	17.52	17.65
8	14.91	15.04	15.17	15.31	15.44	15.57	15.71	15.84	15.98	16.12	16.25
9	13.81	13.94	14.08	14.21	14.35	14.49	14.63	14.76	14.90	15.04	15.18
10	12.94	13.08	13.21	13.35	13.49	13.63	13.78	13.92	14.06	14.20	14.35
11	12.24	12.38	12.52	12.66	12.80	12.95	13.09	13.24	13.38	13.53	13.68
12	11.66	11.81	11.95	12.10	12.24	12.39	12.54	12.68	12.83	12.98	13.13
13	11.19	11.33	11.48	11.63	11.78	11.92	12.08	12.23	12.38	12.53	12.69
14	10.78	10.93	11.08	11.23	11.38	11.54	11.69	11.85	12.00	12.16	12.31
15	10.44	10.59	10.75	10.90	11.05	11.21	11.37	11.52	11.68	11.84	12.00
16	10.15	10.30	10.46	10.62	10.77	10.93	11.09	11.25	11.41	11.57	11.74
17	9.90	10.05	10.21	10.37	10.53	10.69	10.85	11.02	11.18	11.35	11.51
18	9.68	9.84	10.00	10.16	10.32	10.49	10.65	10.82	10.98	11.15	11.32
19	9.49	9.65	9.81	9.98	10.14	10.31	10.47	10.64	10.81	10.98	11.15
20	9.32	9.48	9.65	9.82	9.98	10.15	10.32	10.49	10.66	10.84	11.01
21	9.17	9.34	9.51	9.68	9.85	10.02	10.19	10.36	10.54	10.71	10.89
22	9.04	9.21	9.38	9.55	9.73	9.90	10.07	10.25	10.42	10.60	10.78
23	8.93	9.10	9.27	9.44	9.62	9.79	9.97	10.15	10.33	10.51	10.69
24	8.83	9.00	9.17	9.35	9.52	9.70	9.88	10.06	10.24	10.42	10.60
25	8.74	8.91	9.09	9.26	9.44	9.62	9.80	9.98	10.16	10.35	10.53
26	8.66	8.83	9.01	9.19	9.37	9.55	9.73	9.91	10.10	10.28	10.47
27	8.58	8.76	8.94	9.12	9.30	9.49	9.67	9.85	10.04	10.23	10.41
28	8.52	8.70	8.88	9.06	9.25	9.43	9.61	9.80	9.99	10.18	10.37
29	8.46	8.64	8.82	9.01	9.19	9.38	9.57	9.75	9.94	10.13	10.32
30	8.41	8.59	8.78	8.96	9.15	9.33	9.52	9.71	9.90	10.09	10.29
31	8.36	8.55	8.73	8.92	9.11	9.30	9.48	9.68	9.87	10.06	10.25
32	8.32	8.50	8.69	8.88	9.07	9.26	9.45	9.64	9.84	10.03	10.22
33	8.28	8.47	8.66	8.85	9.04	9.23	9.42	9.61	9.81	10.00	10.20
34	8.25	8.44	8.63	8.82	9.01	9.20	9.39	9.59	9.78	9.98	10.18
35	8.22	8.41	8.60	8.79	8.98	9.18	9.37	9.56	9.76	9.96	10.16
36	8.19	8.38	8.57	8.76	8.96	9.15	9.35	9.54	9.74	9.94	10.14
37	8.16	8.35	8.55	8.74	8.94	9.13	9.33	9.53	9.72	9.92	10.12
38	8.14	8.33	8.53	8.72	8.92	9.11	9.31	9.51	9.71	9.91	10.11
39	8.12	8.31	8.51	8.70	8.90	9.10	9.30	9.50	9.70	9.90	10.10
40	8.10	8.30	8.49	8.69	8.89	9.08	9.28	9.48	9.68	9.88	10.08

Self-Liquidating Mortgages—Monthly Payments
Per Thousand (5-Year Intervals)

Interest Rate	10-Year Loan	15-Year Loan	20-Year Loan	25-Year Loan	30-Year Loan
12-1/4%	$14.49	$12.16	$11.19	$10.72	$10.48
12-1/2	14.64	12.33	11.36	10.90	10.67
12-3/4	14.78	12.49	11.54	11.09	10.87
13	14.93	12.65	11.72	11.28	11.06
13-1/4	15.08	12.82	11.89	11.47	11.26
13-1/2	15.23	12.98	12.07	11.66	11.45
13-3/4	15.38	13.15	12.25	11.85	11.65
14	15.53	13.32	12.44	12.04	11.85
14-1/4	15.68	13.49	12.62	12.23	12.05
14-1/2	15.83	13.66	12.80	12.42	12.25
14-3/4	15.98	13.83	12.98	12.61	12.44
15	16.13	14.00	13.17	12.81	12.64
15-1/4	16.29	14.17	13.35	13.00	12.84
15-1/2	16.44	14.34	13.54	13.20	13.05
15-3/4	16.60	14.51	13.73	13.39	13.25
16	16.75	14.69	13.91	13.59	13.45
16-1/4	16.91	14.68	14.10	13.79	13.65
16-1/2	17.06	15.04	14.29	13.98	13.85
16-3/4	17.22	15.21	14.48	14.18	14.05
17	17.38	15.39	14.67	14.38	14.26
17-1/4	17.54	15.57	14.86	14.58	14.46
17-1/2	17.70	15.75	15.05	14.78	14.66
17-3/4	17.86	15.92	15.24	14.97	14.87
18	18.02	16.10	15.43	15.17	15.07
18-1/4	18.18	16.28	15.63	15.37	15.28
18-1/2	18.34	16.47	15.82	15.57	15.48
18-3/4	18.50	16.65	16.01	15.78	15.68
19	18.67	16.83	16.21	15.98	15.89
19-1/4	18.83	17.01	16.40	16.18	16.09
19-1/2	19.00	17.19	16.60	16.38	16.30
19-3/4	19.16	17.38	16.79	16.58	16.50
20	19.33	17.56	16.99	16.78	16.71